I

AM

THEREFORE

WE

ARE

KRIS PHOTOGRAPHING MAMA AFRIKA IN THE HOUSE WHERE SHE GREW UP IN MDANTSANE IN NOVEMBER 2015

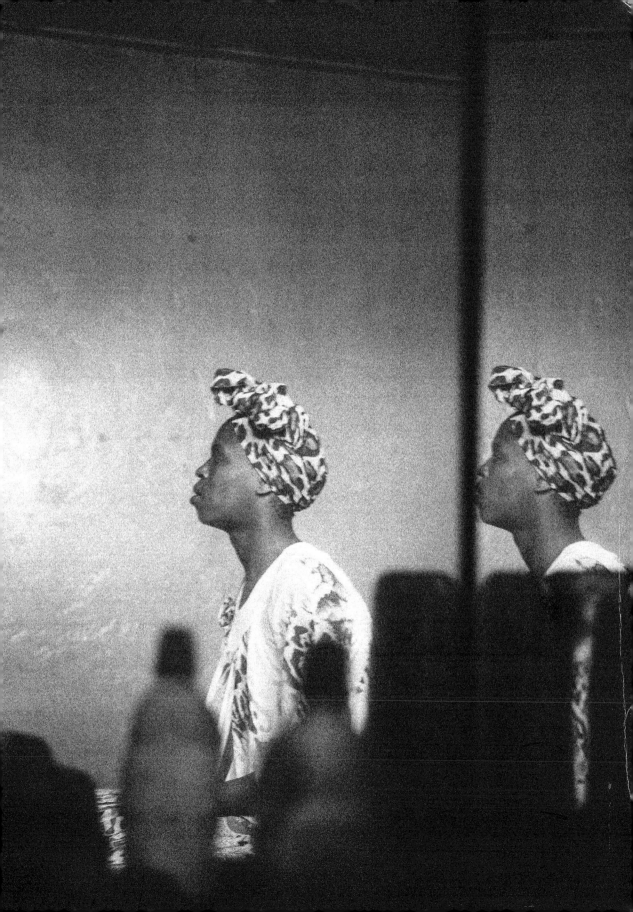

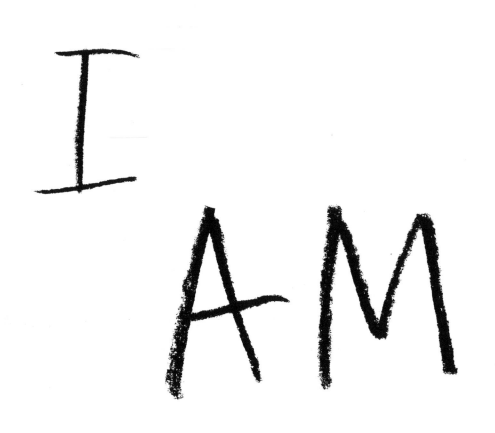

THEREFORE

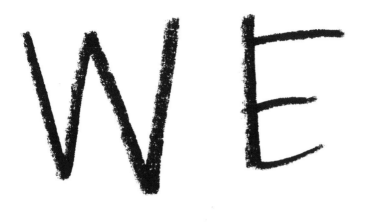

Kris Lyseggen and Herb Schreier

SFINX Publishing
Berkeley, California

SFINX Publishing

www.sfinxus.com

*I Am, Therefore, We Are* is a work of nonfiction. Some names, places, and other identify-
ing information about people may have been changed to protect anonymity.

Book design by Bob Aufuldish, Aufuldish & Warinner, aufwar.com

Library of Congress Control Number: 2017908004

ISBN 978-0-9856244-4-6

eBook ISBN 978-0-9856244-5-3

Printed in the United States

10 9 8 7 6 5 4 3 2 1

# Contents

To Tulie, Thabisa, and Arthur,
who never got to see this book

To Jake, Abby, and Erik

To our Galician, Polish, and Norwegian parents
who instilled in us from the very beginning
a deep sense of gender equality
and a respect for one another as human beings

—Kris Lyseggen and Herb Schreier

# I Am, Therefore, We Are

The belief in a universal bond of sharing that connects all humanity, *I Am, Therefore, We Are*, is one of many ways to describe the philosophy behind the term *Ubuntu*. Many South Africans, like Nelson Mandela and Desmond Tutu, made *Ubuntu* known to the West during and after Apartheid, describing it simply as humanness, showing humanity to others, and togetherness, for without each other we are nothing.

In their own voice, often in what is their second, third, or fourth language, through their transfeminist movement started by some very brave transgender women in the rural areas and townships, these pioneers share the intimate stories about being trans and Xhosa in post-Apartheid South Africa.

We hope that this book will show the extraordinary humanity that we experienced on our trips to the Eastern Cape, the humaneness and hospitality of our new friends and colleagues whom we got to know through S.H.E. (Social, Health, and Empowerment). *Ubuntu*, they explained, was their way of life, deeply rooted in their traditions for generations, across their country and the sub-Saharan African continent.

Unfortunately, the political and systematic failure of their governments to live up to the ideals of their new constitution, one that was based on reconciliation, was failing the very people it was meant to serve after decades of abasement under colonialism:

> *There is a need for understanding but not for vengeance,*
> *a need for reparation but not for retaliation, a need*
> *for ubuntu but not for victimization.*
> —EPILOGUE OF THE INTERIM CONSTITUTION
>   OF SOUTH AFRICA, 1993

We hope that this book will shed some light on what we found most encouraging about the stories they shared with us, that of the incredible resilience among the many young transgender women in one of the most violent places on earth, especially for women but also men, and for LGBT people in particular—a country oftentimes called "The Rape Nation." Violence is the lot of most women throughout the world, but South Africa now must feel like a huge betrayal. After a heroic route toward freedom, perhaps unique in history, one without a bloodbath committed by the oppressed majority, it must feel like an incredible letdown that the country continues to look away from the violence against humans and their humanness. These transwomen constantly demonstrated that through their intelligence, strength, and stubbornness they would not cease to push for the cause of being allowed to be who they are. They call it "Transilience." On our trips to South Africa to record their struggles, we were again and again reminded of their irresistible, interesting culture and history.

In their own words, here are their stories.

—Kris Lyseggen and Herb Schreier
   Berkeley, California 2017

PREVIOUS SPREADS: HERB (LEFT) INTERVIEWING LEIGH ANN VAN DER MERWE (SECOND LEFT) WHILE SHE COOKS DINNER AT

HER HOME THAT SHE SHARES WITH HER OLDER SISTER, WHO IS ILL. HER OTHER SISTER, FELICITY THERESA DE KOCK (RIGHT)

AND ASHLEE LOOTS (FRONT RIGHT) ALSO WORK AT S.H.E. BUFFALO FLATS, NOVEMBER 2015

# Orphans of a Cape Colony

BY KRIS LYSEGGEN

MARCH, 2017

Almost as south as we can be, almost where the Indian and the Atlantic Oceans cross, near the tip of mother Africa, we arrive to the sound of barking, busy critters, screaming speakers, yelling car horns. We see vivacious women in red and yellow and blue. The former black township built during Apartheid is now an urban Xhosa kingdom. But there are no kings in Duncan Village. The kings and the country's president hold court elsewhere.

Now I'm behind the wheel on the "British wrong side" of the road, with Thabisa next to me because it's "safest to show that we are with someone black." We drive through a galvanizing urban wilderness, Herb, my husband, in the back with flashbacks from his last visit some twenty years before, just after Apartheid had ended. There's an uncertainty here, images from a Mad Max dystopia come to mind, as does a series of other movies on lawlessness and bleak, empty futures.

Except Duncan Village is anything but bleak.

Thabisa, a Duncan native, is our guide and translator. This is my first time in South Africa. The sights of the white colonial towns and wine districts do not interest me; we're here to document the rural transgender women, to learn how they juggle the landscape, as they pave the way on the Eastern front in a new transfeminist movement.

As we drive from our B&B in the white, once Dutch colonial city of eMonti (East London), Thabisa guides us through roads so steep that we no longer can see the city after a minute. Down in a bountiful valley of uncontrollable grass, an urbanized savannah, we take a quick left turn to the most densely populated area imaginable: thousands of vulnerable homemade homes, smoke steaming from misplaced pipes; or perhaps it is the tin foil shacks that are on fire. It is chaotic, unruly, and unpredictable. Kids without parents are jumping into skips of container trash to look for treasures, and the villains, Thabisa explains, are hanging out at the odd and rare roundabout. Despite the cacophony of degrading garbage piles, we quickly pick up the *Ubuntu*, their ancestral spirits and traditions of collectiveness, collective crowds of waving Africans, our fore-mothers, who are beaming as they come out of the homes made human from the most inhumane segregation of skin color and ethnicity. A few residents give us uncertain eyebrow-furrows from the dirt road as we pass their makeshift homes that often go up in flames. We're made aware of the proximity to Mandela's birthplace, and listen to the residents' beautiful "click-click" language called isiXhosa.

Now and then when people spot Thabisa in our car, their faces retreat to natural kind wrinkles, shouting Xhosa words we don't understand: "Ndiyabona umntu omhlophe!" (I see a white man!). Thabisa, still in the car, opens the windows wide and touches them gently.

"It looks just like it did during Apartheid," I whisper briskly a few days later during a white tablecloth dinner with our new colleagues at S.H.E. in eMonti.

"The difference is this, Kris. The difference is that we can now sit here with you in this very restaurant and eat together," Thabisa explains while she is fidgeting tenderly with my pony tail. Only two decades earlier, when Thabisa was a child, this would have been illegal. The native black Africans were sepa-rated from the *whites* who had invaded their land. The *coloreds* were separated from the *whites* and the *blacks* and forced into their own separate townships away from the *whites* and the *blacks*.

Their traditions tell of a first leader, King uXhosa, namesake of their clan. Xhosa people are from a Bantu ethnic group of the southern part of Africa, found mainly in what is now called the Eastern Cape. They tried to fight off the European settlers in nine different wars that lasted one hundred years, from 1779 to 1879, often called the Xhosa Wars. Eventually they lost to colonialism and apartheid, as many nations before them. They still have seven kingdoms in South Africa, a king for each of the seven biggest ethnic groups, and eleven different official languages recognized in their constitution. Their current king, King Mendeulo Sigcawu Aah! Zwelenko, was crowned king of AmaXhosa in 2015.

In Duncan Village we visited several other transgender women: Soso, BJ, and Phiwe, always with a clear understanding to tread carefully, as we do not belong here. They live among the eighty thousand or more residents on a few acres of land. Garbage and holes in the streets, unemployed women with large baskets on their heads. In homes we see sparse or no furniture, we see brave and beaten women cleaning and hanging clothes, orphans of AIDS running with sticks and jumping pits, unemployed men looking drunk and destructive.

Duncan becomes less exotic and more familiar as we travel back and forth from our "colonial mansion" to the township of despair and delight.

We venture farther, to eQonce (King Williamstown), eRhini (Grahamstown), eTinarha; (Uitenhage), eBhayi (Port Elisabeth), and Mdantsane. A little deeper into their territories, we can sometimes sense the resistance to the white and to the West. They are proud of their cultures and ways. Some stretch their hands in excitement to wish us welcome, or to ask for bread.

By this time, the fourth president of South Africa, the polygamist Jacob Zuma (a Zulu native), keeps going backward. By now he has almost two dozen children and has married six times. Embroiled in corruption charges for violating the constitution, he never strays far from fraud and controversy that has followed him like a straight line of ants who seek shelter in the rain. On trial for rape, he admits in court that he didn't use a condom when having sex with the woman accusing him of rape, despite knowing that she was HIV positive. But he took

a shower afterward to "cut the risk of contracting HIV," said
the president of the democratic country, who was also the head
of the National AIDS Council at the time. He has so many
love-children that he has little love left for his own people, just
like the men before him, before Mandela and after Mandela.
The "after" president said that HIV does not lead to AIDS. The
Rape Nation, with the most democratic, most humane constitution in the world, did, however, more recently develop a "new
cure." "Rape-a-virgin" will cure you of AIDS. It is increasing in
popularity, up 400 percent since 2002, and right now 50 percent
of all South African children will be raped before the age of
eighteen.

Not much help ever comes their way. Not to Duncan
Village or the other eight or so former townships that we
visited. But many a Duncan native runs proudly around in a
Freebee yellow ANC shirt with a big smiling Mandela face on
their chest. Duncan is a polluted place. Polluted by the white
man. Polluted by human rights abuses, poverty, violence, and
hostility toward people who are transgender, lesbian, and gay.
Badmouthing from a corrupt government with one of the
world's most progressive constitutions, which included equality
for LGBT people from the very beginning. But the mayors and
ombudsmen are still going against the Good Constitution, like
Zuma, who proclaims that same-sex marriage is "a disgrace to
the nation and to God." ("When I was growing up, an ungqin-
gili [a homosexual] would not have stood in front of me. I
would knock him out.")[1]

In the middle of their hustling, hurried lives, we're invited
back to Thabisa's house to meet her family. In this sheltered
shack city we learn that fifteen percent of all residents have HIV.
AIDS orphans are head of their own households and often join
criminal gangs when they are ten or twelve. People sometimes
have electricity, when they run a cable to link up with the power

[1] Anushka Asthana, "PROFILE: Jacob Zuma," *Sunday Times* (London),
December 23, 2007.

The young women explain their fate.

They don't need to prove to us

that they are women.

They don't need high heels and dresses

to prove that they are women.

They don't need to be trapped

in the hierarchy of men

on the patriarchal continent

that is Africa.

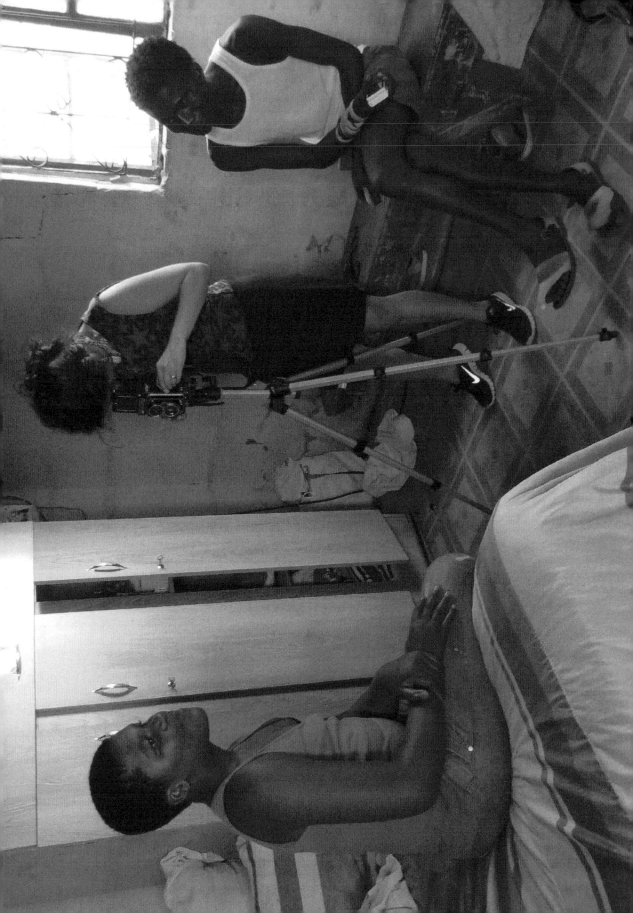

box that is serving the entire village. They have no water in their homes. "People are starving," Thabisa says. People are dying of AIDS and tuberculosis. The HIV medicine eats up the insides of their hungry stomachs. Thabisa's mother, a full-time maid in another town, is home for the weekend. At least ten of Thabisa's relatives join us in the small living room, which is also the bedroom and the kitchen. They're struggling with everything that is the endemic and epidemic of despair and lives cut short in Duncan Village. Thabisa's sister, and best friend, also Thabisa, takes off her head scarf and shows us a deep hole in her head. She dies a few months later.

On our next trip, Herb and I drive on the wrong side, alone, to find Thabisa's new house, proud as one can be for finding it without a map, more difficult than driving in a ten-lane highway or the streets of Bangkok.

Duncan has become worse since our first year, Thabisa explains. She says that we should no longer travel alone in the car without a black person. Duncan Village has become hostile and dangerous even for people who live there. And a white man, a plumber; has just been killed, while he was doing some work in the village. Transgender and gay people are being stabbed and beaten. Nobody knows how many have died. The police don't want to know how many have been stabbed and beaten.

Sometimes it's hard to see if the clouds and tornadoes of gray exhausted smoke come from the makeshift barbecues, smoking guns, burning flesh or tires, or from the flames that burn the vulnerable people and their shelters to the ground.

We visit more women. We smile at the soon-to-be familiar requiem of the good grandmother who never had a problem with her granddaughter being born with male genitals. We smile knowingly to the thought of the antimisogynist grandmothers.

As soon as the women warriors learn who we are, they almost always invite us in. The young women explain their fate. They don't need to prove to us that they are women. They don't

KRIS IS PHOTOGRAPHIG BJ IN DUNCAN VILLAGE IN APRIL 2014 WITH THABISA (RIGHT) TRANSLATING FROM XHOSA. PHOTO: HERB SCHREIER

need high heels and dresses to prove that they are women. They don't need to be trapped in the hierarchy of men on the patriarchal continent that is Africa. (By the end of this project, two of the women we met have already died, gone forever.) They are women like all women in jeans and T-shirts. They are women like all women, with goals and dreams and wanderlust. Inside their homes, in their personal space, they offer us knowledge, water, and curiosity. We record the young women's voices, tell them that we will give back in the form of this book, hand it to them and thank them, their families present in crowded rooms, their personal stories added to history, their raped and killed friends not far from their consciousness, their resilience saved on hard drives and discussed each night during our stay, stored safely in our gated, colonial bedroom.

I'M LOVING IT OUT

# I'm Loving It Out

## ASHLEE LOOTS

BUFFALO FLATS, eMONTI (EAST LONDON)

You asked about cultural religion. It takes me back to a time
when I was eighteen years old. It was a very bad time in my life.
It was a time where suicide was the only thing I could think
about. It was a time when you wanted to express the inner person, when you want to be yourself, when you want to explore,
when you want to learn. And it was a time when I went to
visit my aunt. My aunt had this friend over. She was a spiritual
psychologist from some church. And we had this conversation.
I told her that this is how I see myself; I see myself as a woman.
I've never identified with the male context. I never loved my life
as male. I've been feminine all my life. And she listened very,
very, very carefully to my story, and then she replied, "You know
you have dealt with this in a former life." What I was going
through, she said, was the spirit of confusion. It was the spirit of
the Nile, she said. I was tricked in the spirit of confusion, and
I didn't know who I was. And she advised me to love according
to the law of the Bible.

The Bible says this and that, but what about me? How can
I live a life according to the standards of man when I never felt
like a man? She advised me that dating men was wrong.

I can now truly say that I am in this part of my life where
I'm loving it out. No matter how people find it disgraceful, I
love myself. I accept myself, and I love it to the fullest. I believe
there is a greater judge, and he shall judge us all. And I always
tell that to people. You judge me now, but I had to stand before
a greater judge, and I have to give answers according to what
I've done in my life. Only God does all that.

## Rodney dies

One thing that really changed me was when my friend Rodney
got stabbed. She got stabbed in the neck by a seventeen-year-old

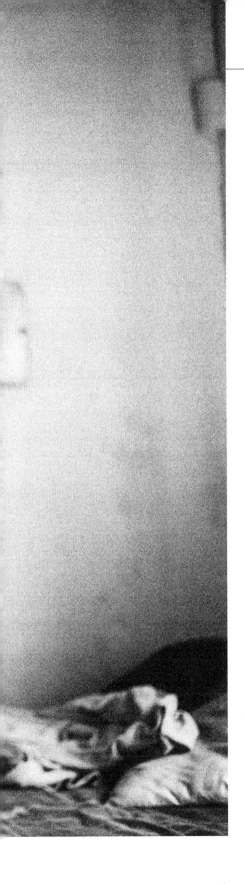

ASHLEE LOOTS PREPARING FOR OUR INTERVIEW. ASHLEE IS A TRANSFEMINIST INTERN AT S.H.E. AND COMES FROM KIMBERLY NEAR JOHANNESBURG. BUFFALO FLATS, NOVEMBER 2015.

boy. She never knew that she was trans, but everybody could see that she was a woman. She had her own little place. She was just a woman through and through. She had no children, she had no one but herself. So that Saturday when she was stabbed, near where I was staying, my cousin called me and told me to come over: "Rodney has been stabbed."

And when I got there, they put that silver thing on her. She was dead. She was no more. And I said to myself, I will never die like Rodney has just died. It's either that I love my life to the fullest or I would have to end it at the hands of these people who are so merciless. And that guy [went] free. He never went to prison. There was no evidence, no witness, no one. My friend never got justice for her case. She was my closest friend. I never got a time to mourn her death because there was so much politics, so much complexness. Nobody really acknowledged her because everyone knew in the community she was just another "mofee." Rodney . . . my only friend I could talk to about who I was and who I really wanted to be.

Her death has driven me. It has really driven me to just stand in this movement, to be vocal, and to speak to my other sisters because I don't want the same thing to happen to them, what happened to Rodney. We die at the hands of our lovers, of our perpetrators, yet they walk around freely.

## Mr. HIV

A few months ago I told this story to my doctor. I don't usually talk about it that much. It's a beautiful story. I called the story "how the strangers saved me from HIV." Sometimes I call it "Mr. HIV." I think we trans people are always on trial. If we are not on trial with our lovers, it's a trial with our family. If it's not the trial with our family, it's a trial with ourselves, with our inner being. We are just always in a struggle. If not in a struggle with ourselves, it's a struggle with the next girl.

It was a beautiful night. And I met one of my friends. We used to go to the same church together. She was like, "Hi!" I

Her death has driven me.

It has really driven me

to just stand in this movement,

to be vocal,

and to speak to my other sisters

because I don't want the same thing

to happen to them,

what happened to Rodney.

We die at the hands of our lovers,

of our perpetrators,

yet they walk around freely.

hadn't seen her in a long time, and I said, "Hi!" You know how
[it is] with girls and friends who haven't seen each other in a
long time. We danced all night long. And then this guy turns
up. We danced together. And we started kissing. I asked him,
"Let's hear it, what's your name?" I introduced him to my friend,
and she said, "This is my cousin!" I was like, "It's your cousin?
How nice!" And we danced the rest of the night, and then he
said to me, "Let's go out." We went behind this building not far
away from the club. We went behind the building and started
to talk, and the strangest thing for me was when we were in the
club, I had given him an opportunity to touch me, that's what
I usually do. And I got a sense that he knew. And he had asked
me, "Are you a mofee?" I was like, "Do I look like a mofee to
you?" He said "No." I said "Okay."

So behind the building, I said, "Then, we just have to do
it, do you have a condom?" He said "No." The debates went
on about the condom. And because I haven't had a boyfriend
in a long time, he made me feel good. He made me feel loved
and wanted again. That's what happened. I felt affirmed, I
felt wanted, I felt needed, I felt appreciated, something that I
haven't felt in a long time. And just as he was about to enter me,
penetrate me, whatever the case was, some strangers came along,
these street kids, and they were like, "What are you doing?"
And we stopped immediately. I stood up and I pulled on my
pants and I walked away.

The beautiful thing about that night was, what if those
guys, those street kids, had found out that we were both guys?
Because when they saw us, they thought this was a man and
a woman. Something bad could have happened to both of us.
Many times, my friends have told me some terrible stories about
what happened to them when guys caught them with another
guy. They will beat you and they will expose you.

And I was so lucky that night because they did nothing
to me. They could have raped me as well. I just pulled up my
pants and walked away. I went back into the club to get my

friend and told her what happened. She asked me, "Are you hurt? Are you safe?" And I said, "I'm fine and I'm okay." And then, the week after, I met her again, my friend from the club. I was like, "Girl, how are you? How is your cousin doing?" She said, "Sweetheart, I have to tell you something, but it's a rumor. I only heard it. He is HIV positive."

I was like, "Sweetheart, why are you telling me now? Why?"

"Do you know his ex-girlfriend?" she said. "Rumor has it that she died of HIV."

I felt my world crumbling down. But I knew that he hadn't really penetrated me because, as the sex was about to continue, that street kid had arrived. He caught us in a moment of weakness, in a moment of heat. And I was so afraid now. What if the guy had penetrated me and come inside me? I would have become HIV positive.

And I wasn't ready to become another victim of a one-night stand, because that has happened to my friends, that has happened to my sisters. Because they needed to feel wanted and loved and a guy comes along. What do we do? Luckily my test came back negative. From that night onward, I decided to take responsibility for what's mine. This body is mine. I stand solidly and fully for it. What happens to this body is my choice. So I have decided to take care of my body and respect it, because if I don't respect this body, no one else will.

A trans woman I know once said, "There is nothing like a fresh piece of meat." Guys are like dogs, men are like dogs. They can smell it. And I've experienced it over and over and over again. But I decided to be cautious. I cannot speak of feminism, I cannot speak of woman's rights, I cannot speak of taking care of myself if I am making the wrong choices. Giving my body away like it's for free. I've decided to own up to who I am because no one else will.

—November 2015

# MAMA AFRIKA

# Mama Afrika
## MAMA AFRIKA (LAZOLA CANZIBE)
MDANTSANE, EASTERN CAPE

I want to tell you the story because sometimes when I'm alone, I think of this life that
I used to have, it makes me feel so bad. But
when I'm telling people about it, it heals me.
So that's why I want to tell you the story.

I grew up in this house where I had to
start work at four in the morning. I would
have to cook for the dogs, cook for the pigs,
and then I was forced to eat with the dogs
outdoors. If I did something silly, just like
any child would do, I would get beaten so
bad [by my aunt] that I bled massively.

Her husband is a drunk. When I came
home from school, I got beaten. I had to
wash the dishes, the food was eaten by them,
and then I had to wash the dishes. But there
was no food for me. And then they would
tell me not to go to school, and then I would
be left at home to take care of my little sister.
I told myself that by 1999, I am going to
leave this place.

In 1999 I left, in search of my biological
parents. I went to look for my parents, and
I found them. We stayed together until they
died of old age. Now, I live with another
aunt and her husband. They are my family
now. That's the end of my story.

—November 2015

MAMA AFRIKA SHOWS US WHERE

SHE GREW UP IN MDANTSANE IN

NOVEMBER 2015

THE BACKYARD WHERE MAMA AFRIKA WAS FORCED TO SLEEP WITH THE DOGS AT NIGHT

MAMA AFRIKA IN THE KITCHEN OF HER CHILDHOOD HOME. SHE GREW UP WITH HER AUNT

(LEFT) WHO SHE SAID TREATED HER VERY BADLY. MDANTSANE, NOVEMBER 2015

# THE TRANSFEMINIST

# PIONEER

# The Transfeminist Pioneer
## LEIGH ANN VAN DER MERWE

eMonti (east london)

I could say that I've been loved. I think coming out as transgender and accepting it for myself has been the biggest accomplishment for me because I was also able to tell partners I'm trans. I gave them the choice whether to be in the relationship or not. There are some men I've met who are open to the idea of dating a trans woman, but I cannot say that it's always been uphill. My biggest problem is that I see myself as a feminist, and I don't want men to see me as a sexual object. I don't want anybody to objectify me. The minute I get that feeling, you're out of my life, and that, sadly, is kind of the typical thing in South Africa. I'm supposed to be this woman; I'm supposed to be submissive; I'm supposed to do this and that and the other, but I'm a woman who has a job. I work for myself. I support my family, and my family supports me. Beyond that, I don't think I need anything else. Maybe intimacy, yes, but if the intimacy comes with misogyny, I would rather not have it.

The worst thing to be in South Africa is a trans woman. I think the trans women have accepted the fact that they cannot access health care. They cannot change it, so they have accepted it as the reality. These trans women are not referring to themselves as gay. When they talk, they say, "I'm a woman." They don't even say, "I'm a trans woman."

I have taught these women. I'm not imposing any of this on them, but I have told these women right from the beginning if we're talking about gender, gender is not clothes. Gender is what you feel and how you shape that gender. A lot of them do not wear feminine clothes. They refuse, because that is the very thing that oppresses them in their communities. Being a trans woman in the rural community, you walk down the road with heels; it exposes you to so many forms of violence because even some cabdrivers would not let you get in the cab. A trans

PHILADELPHIA, USA, SEPTEMBER 2014: WE CAME BY LEIGH ANN'S HOTEL ROOM AT SEVEN IN THE MORNING TO CHAT WITH HER AND TAKE SOME PHOTOS BEFORE SHE WAS TO PRESENT AT THE PHILADELPHIA TRANS-HEALTH CONFERENCE

woman was beat up the other day for emulating women's behavior. The public transport system, I think, in our region of South Africa, is the most violent place for trans women.

In South Africa, the flip side to that coin is that you transition into the inequalities of women. Because I'm a woman, I cannot take certain decisions in my family; and because I'm a woman, I am ten times more likely to be raped in South Africa. South Africa is one of the countries with the highest forms of violence against women for a country that is not even post-conflict. That's why I'm always saying to the women: "We must transition with a feminist consciousness, with a consciousness of our bodies and our lives and our rights, and what is intrinsically linked to that is autonomy and agency of our bodies."

The highest priority for us is the burden of HIV among trans women. Second to that is a general health context. Somebody might be HIV positive, but because she's experiencing that disconnect between body and soul, my body is not aligned to who I truly am; I'm not going to take care of it. That's the theory on which I am building. They're not taking care of [themselves]. They would sleep with men, reinfect themselves. What does that mean for the city, for account of a person who, in addition to all of this, is taking alcohol, is smoking weed, is taking drugs, and engaging in very risky and dangerous practices.

I was born and bred in the rural Eastern Cape, a small town called Ugie. My mom died when I was two. I lived with my grandmother and five sisters, four sisters before me, and I come from a family of twelve kids. I'm the last born. And there's been all sorts of theories of why I was so feminine, and a lot of people who met me would also say, "You should have been a girl." A lot of my father's friends said, "You should have been a girl." I stayed with my grandmother, and when I turned nine, she passed away, and I then lived with an aunt, and I stayed with her until I had to go to high school.

It was around that time that one of my sisters got married, and I moved to the neighborhood where she lived with her husband, and we were a few living at that house along with my father. A lot of people would also tell me, "Oh, your father didn't beat you enough; that's why you were so feminine," or "Your father just didn't take an interest in you; that's why you were so feminine," and things like that. I've always known I wanted to have a transition. I always felt different.

When this friend from Johannesburg came to visit, she said to me, "You know, if you take contraceptive pills, you can get your boobs to grow." I started taking these contraceptive pills. It was also around the time my sister got married, and she went off the pill in order to have a baby, and I just started stealing them from home. Then friends were doing favors for me. They would take hormones from the clinic for me, contraceptive pills, and I did that; and when I got to pass fairly, I could do that myself. In the year 1999, my sister was killed by a lover, and with that sadness came the opportunity to move to Cape Town.

I was privileged to go to high school. I was working hard. That was my leverage for dealing with teachers and dealing with bullies, because I worked hard. Academically, I did well because that also afforded me protection from the teachers. So I got the opportunity to move to Cape Town, and from there, I just slowly started phasing into my transition. Little by little, I started using more perfumes, more lotions, a different shoe, a subtle transition. I finished my last two years of high school in Cape Town.

Relationships have always been very difficult for me because there's that "coming out" element, where you have to disclose yourself to guys. I met somebody very dear at university, and he found out that I was not a woman by societal standards, and he left, and I've never looked at relationships the same. This was in 2002 when I was doing my second year at university.

My family has always been very supportive. When I eventually came out and said, "I'm transitioning," I think they sort

We must transition with

a feminist consciousness,

with a consciousness of our bodies

and our lives

and our rights,

and what is intrinsically linked to that

is autonomy and

agency of our bodies.

of rolled their eyes to say, "Oh, my God, finally it's happened," because I think they've always had this idea. I have a very good relationship with my sisters. I'm fortunate. I'm also having a very good relationship with my brother, but it's not been smooth sailing all along. Once I heard my late brother outside entertaining friends and people were asking about his family, and he said, "Well, we have so many sisters and we have so many brothers, and then there's one 'mofee.'" This is the derogatory name for a gay person in South Africa. It made me very sad, but I was also realistic to the realities of being a trans person in South Africa and coming from the rural areas. I developed a peptic ulcer at the age of twelve for which I ended up in hospital.

I was severely stressed throughout high school, and I suffered depression at university. I have had to deal with loss in my family so many times. I cannot describe the kind of numbness that comes when another person dies, and you've just got to accept it, and you've got to get on with life. There's just too many things to focus on. There's school, there's family, there's safety, there's trauma; throughout every loss, I have had to shape myself and to make myself strong and to get on with life.

## Heartache and discrimination

I remember this one incident in Cape Town, it was around my first week at university, and I was just going through so much at that time because the first week I got to university my father passed away, and he was living here in East London. I couldn't come back for the funeral, but I remember these guys were sitting on the corner, and they were friends with some of my schoolmates at the school that I was attending, and they were like, "Is that a guy? Is that a girl? What's happening with that person?" I had just got my student card, and it said "female." I had convinced the person who was registering me to write "female" because it made my life easier on the university campus. I walked up to them, and I just threw the card at them. They read the card for themselves, and of course, they were

LEIGH ANN MEETING NCESHI VENA OUTSIDE NCESHI'S HOME IN PEACE VILLAGE. LEIGH ANN'S COLLEAGUES THANDILE KANTLONI AND PHIWE NGCENGI IN THE BACKGROUND. KWANOBUHLE, NOVEMBER 2015

apologetic; and I took the card, and I walked right off.

As I walked on, I reflected on it, and I thought that was very brave, but it was also very stupid because I exposed myself to violence. They could easily have beaten the hell out of me on that open field. I have had very abusive boyfriends, physically and emotionally. I have suffered from post-traumatic stress. I've been discriminated against.

My resilience comes from that context. It comes from that heartache and that discrimination, where you are so scared and so stressed. I have had an experience where I went to the bank; I applied for a bank account. You give your identity document. It doesn't match what is on the computer, and then you have to come out. I remember she went behind the screen, and she fetched colleagues, and I could see people coming to peek at who is sitting there. So she must have told them the story.

This is why the work I do is so personal to me. It comes from a space of resilience; it comes from a space of oppression; it comes from a space where I just had to resist certain things in my life. When I was a waitress at university, I worked with a white man, and he was the most homophobic/transphobic person I ever met. And I remember this one evening we were sitting in the back of the restaurant where I worked, and one of the other female waitresses, she was telling me about the difficulty with her boyfriends and why are men like this, the "men are pigs" kind of conversation; and he walked into the bar and he pointed to me and said, "You should know men are like that." So in a sense, he was saying, "You're a man. You should understand these things." When I reported him to the management, he became so violent to me. In the morning when I would come to work, he would look at me all funny, and he had all sorts of funny comments around me.

## Didn't want to be out

After university, I came back home to the Eastern Cape in the rural province, and I worked at a security management company, and I was seeking medical services in Pretoria at one of the hospitals there. I met a trans woman who was really fired up about getting human rights for trans people, and at that time, I just thought, "What is this person all about?" I just want to transition and get on with my life. She said to me, "There is this woman in Cape Town who started a project, and I think we should talk to her about getting rights." But I refused to be an activist. I didn't want to be out. I didn't want to love my life. I just wanted to be a woman, and the dream for me was to have a boyfriend or a partner and get on with life.

Once this organization was set up in Cape Town, I had problems with my identity document, and I wrote to the director of the organization, and she said to me, "Okay, according to the interpretations of the Act, you can have the name change even if you are presurgery." And that was music to my ears because I was a university graduate. I worked for something like $150 a month, and it was difficult. There are other people who are unemployed, but I just felt that there's no justice in being a university graduate, and then you work for a security management company. And so I e-mailed this lady, and she said, "Let's see what we can do about this ID situation."

I went to Cape Town. When we got to Home Affairs in Cape Town where I'm supposed to change my ID, the woman said, "I will not take this letter because it does not have the words 'final surgery' on it." I had traveled twenty-two hours to Cape Town on a bus, had gone to see a psychiatrist; the psychiatrist gave me the letter, the same psychiatrist who treated me years ago when I first started my transition, and I was just too tired to be arguing with anyone. And so I came back home and in this rural village called Ngcobo, I gave my paperwork, and the people there were so accommodating and so kind.

LEIGH ANN INVITED US FOR A HOME COOKED MEAL. SHE TAKES CARE OF HER SISTER, WHO IS ILL (MIDDLE). HER SISTER FELICITY THERESA DE KOCK (RIGHT) IS THE OFFICE ADMINISTRATOR AT S.H.E. BUFFALO FLATS, NOVEMBER 2015

They didn't understand trans issues, of course, but they said, "Oh my goodness, you've been going through this all your life. How do you travel? Do you have a job?" You know, people were concerned.

And at that point, I knew that the rural context in which trans people find themselves is a very, very problematic one. That woman who was in Cape Town where there's supposed to be enlightenment and there's supposed to be knowledge out there, she was so stubborn, and that's why I always say that sometimes ignorance is bliss because the person who is ignorant is willing to open themselves up to be educated on the topic. But this woman, she was just speaking from a place where she knew everything, and she wasn't going to take this application. I went to this village; I handed in my application, I got there over the lunch hour. People were drinking Coke. They offered me a Coca-Cola. I did the fingerprints, and off my application went. It took almost two years, but I was able to change it. But it was in that moment where I realized that I have to do something.

I just knew I had to get into activism. I was in my job for two years after that still, but I kept commuting wherever there was an activist space. The first time outside the country for me was Namibia, and trans activists gathered there; and I got so fired up, because I'd been exposed to different people doing different activist work, Gender DynamiX, that was doing this work in South Africa, and it was the first organization to be doing exclusive trans work on the continent.

I had a mentor who took me under his wing, Mr. Robert Hamblin, and I just have such tremendous respect for him. And a lot of the work that I do today was really shaped by what he taught me as an activist, he formed me.

## We were dying

I had a meeting with the regional women in Africa, and we said that trans men have been at the forefront of this movement for so long. What is it that we are doing for ourselves? We went to many meetings, and we realized that we were dying; that trans women are dying from HIV; that trans women are being killed in violent attacks. We need to do something.

So myself and Beyonce from Uganda and Christina from Botswana got together and we spoke, and we had wine, and we were talking, and we had a meeting, and I was just fired up. That meeting combined with the meeting I had in Pretoria—when I got back to East London, I wrote the founding document for the organization, and then I met incredible women in my own network. I met Zaza; I met Soso. We didn't have a blue penny, and it took us three years to get the first funding. Time went on, and we got an office that we paid from only-God-knows-with, sometimes a little bit here, sometimes a little bit there. People came to that office dedicated to this mission like they were paid a salary at the end of the month. They came at 8:00 in the morning, and they left at 5:00 in the afternoon, women like Zaza, Thabisa, Phiwe; they were always there. [In that space] we had different platforms where we could talk about things.

We applied to a feminist fund, and we thought they probably won't give us money because there's feminist politics out there that trans women are not women, and they probably won't give us a dime, but what the heck. Let's do it. So over the Christmas period, I was writing this proposal for $2,000 US, it's a South African funder. And I remember being in Namibia the following year; it was around March—March or May. We submitted the application in January, and in May they called us to say we are giving you this to set yourselves up. We thought heaven and earth of this money because we didn't have a dime, and we had nowhere to turn to.

There was such pressure from my family—"You are educated. Why in God's name are you doing this? You can have a job in the bank . . ."—but I didn't want a job in the bank. I needed to work with these women who are so resilient and who resisted these oppressions in so many ways by the way they were

LEIGH ANN'S MOTHER PASSED AWAY WHEN LEIGH ANN WAS TWO YEARS OLD. HERE, A RARE PHOTO OF BOTH HER PARENTS IN UGIE WHERE LEIGH ANN WAS BORN. ONE OF HER SISTERS WAS KILLED BY HER SISTER'S LOVER IN 1999. LEIGH ANN HAS 10 MORE SIBLINGS, MANY OF WHOM HAVE PASSED AWAY, TOO

I have started thinking

about transformative practices,

so the trans in transfeminism

for me is not necessarily

about transgender feminism

but transformative practice.

I think feminism itself is a label,

and any label

has the potential of being stifling.

It can overwhelm you.

talking, by the way they were walking down the road. Zaza is one of the most resistant women I know. She is tall with high heels. People look back and stare at her. She just keeps going; and that, for me, is the ultimate resistance of oppression.

One of the heartbreaking facts for me was many feminists accuse trans women of having some sort of privilege. If you go into Duncan Village and you look at where these trans women live, then I ask you to look in my eyes, and where is this privilege?

Once there was a training by a well-known feminist, and they put out an application for this training, and one of the requirements was that you had to be female born, and you have to live in the category of women, whatever that might mean, and that you had to identify yourself as a woman. And we challenged this. We wrote to them. We said, "What's up with these criteria? What is a woman? Explain that to us. Because you claim that gender is a social construction and that gender is not determined by birth." Of course, they didn't really write back to us, except for a very brief response to say that they will take up this conversation at a board level and blah, blah, blah.

We never got a real response from them, and we took it a step farther. We said, "Let's write an open letter to them and put the issue out there in the public so we can create dialogue." It really stimulated dialogue, but the problem that we have in South Africa is that we have worked with mainstream women's organizations and mainstream feminist organizations, and they are more welcoming than the lesbian radical feminists. Those are the people who exclude us, and it's kind of sad because we would think they understand our struggle and where we come from, but those are the people who are really gatekeeping the feminist spaces. It was nothing but transphobia.

—April 2014

A YEAR LATER

## Transformative

For me, initially, when I started talking about transfeminism, I started looking at it in a way that feminism addresses trans issues or trans women's issues. However, I have started thinking about transformative practices, so the trans in trans feminism for me is not necessarily about transgender feminism but transformative practice. I think feminism itself is a label, and any label has the potential of being stifling. It can overwhelm you. It can get boring at times; and so for me, I think the focus of my work is really to build a transformative practice, in literature, but also in practice. There's very little literature about trans feminism, about the way that the two intersect—transgender and feminism.

But I'm more interested in looking at feminism from the lens of marginalized women, feminism on the practice of women of disability, HIV positive women, people of color. I don't think that there's a role for everyone in feminism. I think men are supporters of feminism, and I think they can identify themselves as feminists, too. Though the feminist movement is really grounded in women's issues, but I don't think men have a big role to play.

I do think that trans people have a big role to play. I think that the gender-nonconforming have a big role to play in trying to understand what this means. I'm interested in transformative behavior. I've been on the margins of feminism, and I've had to fight for my place in the sun, so to speak. So I'm not interested any more in being recognized as a feminist. If people give me that recognition, great; but if I can transform this stifling behavior, this gender policing, then I feel I've done my job.

South African initiatives around social change have always been very community driven. The revolution has really come from the crowd, from the people. In South Africa, we've learned that if something doesn't go our way in society, we take it to the

FEMINISTS ON THE ROAD: LEIGH ANN WITH HER FRIEND AND COLLEAGUE NACHALE (HUA) BOONYAPISOMPARN. THEY ARE CONSTANTLY PRESENTING THEIR WORK AROUND THE GLOBE TO RAISE AWARENESS OF TRANS ISSUES, TO CHALLENGE OUR PERCEPTION OF WHAT A 'REAL WOMAN' IS AND TO CHALLENGE THE RADICAL 'ANTI-TRANS' FEMINIST MOVEMENT. PHILADELPHIA, SEPTEMBER 2014

It's really important to acknowledge

that as trans women,

we are not gay people,

we are not women with dicks,

we are not sexually factitious,

we are just good old women . . .

and because we are women,

we suffer multiple layers of oppression

and discrimination.

streets, and I think that's where most of the innovation comes from. It's really from the streets. When we started this organization, we knew that we had a problem with mainstream feminism and the way that it's talking about women and women's rights. And slowly, we're starting to transform that. There has been an African Transformative Feminist Leadership Institute that was conducted by [us]. That is the first on the African continent.

The Leadership Institute was really my conceptualization. It was a space where we brought together trans women from eight African countries in eastern, southern Africa where we talked about what does feminism mean to us. How is it that we are going to advance a feminist agenda on the continent? We had three days in which we sat down, we deliberated, we had different sessions, we had different panels. And what we did leave with was the fact that we have written a charter that is going to be published by Duke University in the States. It's called the African Trans Feminist Charter, and we left with at least three goals for ourselves over the next two or three years about advancing trans women's voices in feminist discourse.

It's really unfortunate that when these things happen, that it always has to happen in South Africa. Because of the fear of safety and security issues in other African countries, there's a lot of gender policing in African states; for example, when a trans woman arrives in Zimbabwe who is fem, who looks female, presents as female, and has an ID that says male, there's the possibility of violence, the possibility of incarceration, arrest, it could end up being a nightmare.

## Beyond breasts and the vagina

Let me start by saying there's a political will to address the issues of LGBT people. However, there's a lack of understanding of my dynamics and my issues as a trans woman when I'm going to report it at a police station where there is a police officer who was raised in a very heteronormative world, in a Christian society probably, grappling to understand what is my issue because he will see me as a man in a dress when I really identify myself as a woman.

There are some things that the government is doing. There's a task team that is aimed at dealing with cases of hate violence, but I don't think that there's room for sensitization. What we've done as an organization was to start talking to people at the very fundamentals of gender. And later in the conversation, we bring in gender diversity, give them an entry point to the conversation that says gender is not as fixed as we would like to think it is. I think that has worked well. It is yet to be seen whether there is an increase or a decline in hate crimes. My feeling is there's an increase, I also feel like a lot of cases are not reported because there's no trust in the system.

It's really important to acknowledge that as trans women, we are not gay people, we are not women with dicks, we are not sexually factitious, we are just good old women. I think we can transcend these thoughts of the body and how we police the body. I think there's a way of looking at womanhood beyond the breast and the vagina and the hips, and so I think women come in different shapes. It's very important for women to acknowledge, first of all, that we are women, and because we are women, we suffer multiple layers of oppression and discrimination.

—November 2015

TO GO TO THE MOUNTAIN

# To Go To The Mountain

## PHIWE NGCINGI

DUNCAN VILLAGE, EASTERN CAPE

IN HER OWN WRITING

### The scar

Last year, on October 15, 2015, we went to the Tavern, me and
my friend Austin. I bought some beers while we were just cooling
ourselves outside. One man approached me, and I went to the
washroom with him. He asked for my number, I gave it to him.
Then on my way back to Austin, three women asked me what
I had been doing with Themba in the washroom. I told them
he asked for my number. While I said this, one woman threw a
beer bottle at me. I bled a lot. Then when I looked up, I saw lots
of guys were standing there saying I should be beaten more. We
looked for assistance from any car passing by, but no one wanted
to take me to the hospital. We had to call a cab to the hospital.

I arrived at the hospital, but the nurses didn't want to stitch
me. Finally they gave in and stitched me, but they stitched me
all wrong.

PHIWE IS SHOWING US THE SCAR THAT SHE GOT AFTER FIRST BEING ATTACKED WITH A GLASS BOTTLE IN A BAR BY SEVERAL WOMEN, AND THEN HOW THE DOCTORS DID NOT DO A GOOD JOB OF STITCHING HER UP AFTERWARDS. DUNCAN VILLAGE, NOVEMBER 2015

## The rape

It was on April 17, 2014, when I received a call from my friend Anele Klasman. He asked me to come with him to town, as it was [the] weekend and there would be lots of fun. I quickly bathed, got dressed, and went to meet him. It was very boring there, so we walked to a tavern and started drinking through the night, entertaining ourselves with dancing, and we got very drunk. On our way to "California Club" we bumped into three men who asked what time it was, but we ignored them and kept walking. One of them came after me and started touching me while the others searched my friend and found his phone. Shortly thereafter, they came on to me, searched me as well for my phone, and I got irritated. I attempted to fight them, but they were too strong. I was outnumbered. They beat me, took my money. I took hold of my phone and threw it to the ground so that it would break. I was thinking that if I couldn't have it, no one else should. This made them very angry, and they took me to their car, drove off with me to an empty school, started brutally raping me. They spent the whole night taking turns, threw themselves inside me like I was a piece of sponge, until the early hours of the morning. One of the men repeatedly kissed me on the lips. Then I got kicked out of their car, and [I] watched them leave. I was weak and pained. Despite the state I was in, I managed to take the number plate and dragged my numb body to my friend's place, where I spent the night. With the companion of a friend, I went to the police station to report it. They asked what the problem was, and I explained every-thing. The police then took me to the hospital, where all the medical procedures where rape is concerned were taken. Then they took me for counseling.

## The dream

I was born in Mdantsane. My parents died when I was little, and I grew up with my aunts in Duncan Village. My dream when I was growing up was, I could see myself as a teacher. Now I want to become a psychologist to assist the transgender people here. Transgender people are the people who face the most violence, especially on the Eastern Cape, because people here do not know anything about gender identity. They only have the stereotyped minds, that this child is a boy. I'm expected to get a wife and expected to go to the Mountain [to be circumcised], and I am expected to do all the things men are doing. My dream is to be able to see a free world, where transgender people are free to express themselves, where I can be a woman like any woman. That we can get jobs and have an income. Most transgender people here cannot get a job, and many have been chased away from their homes. I want our communities in South Africa to understand us and treat us like human beings.

—November 2015

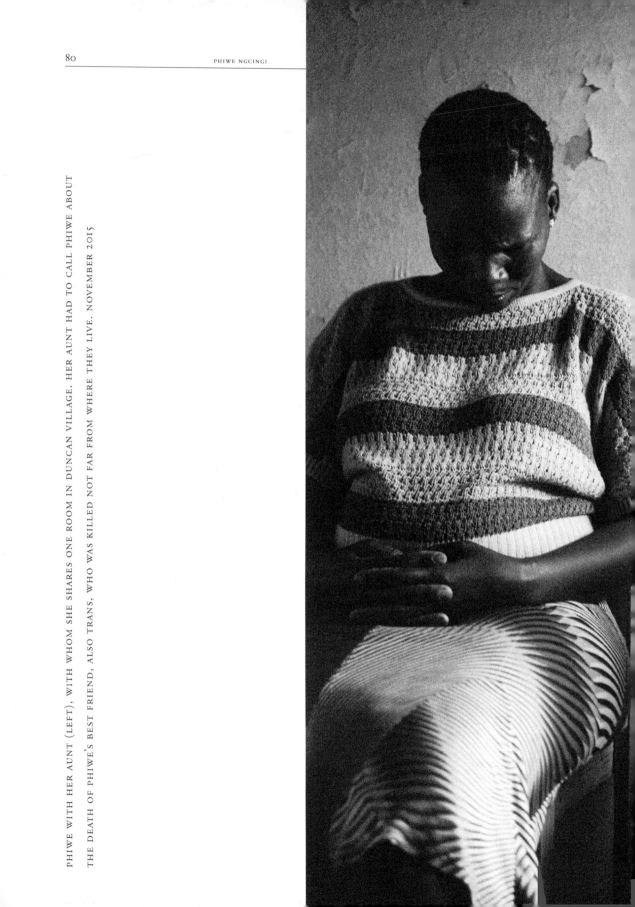

PHIWE WITH HER AUNT (LEFT), WITH WHOM SHE SHARES ONE ROOM IN DUNCAN VILLAGE. HER AUNT HAD TO CALL PHIWE ABOUT THE DEATH OF PHIWE'S BEST FRIEND, ALSO TRANS, WHO WAS KILLED NOT FAR FROM WHERE THEY LIVE. NOVEMBER 2015

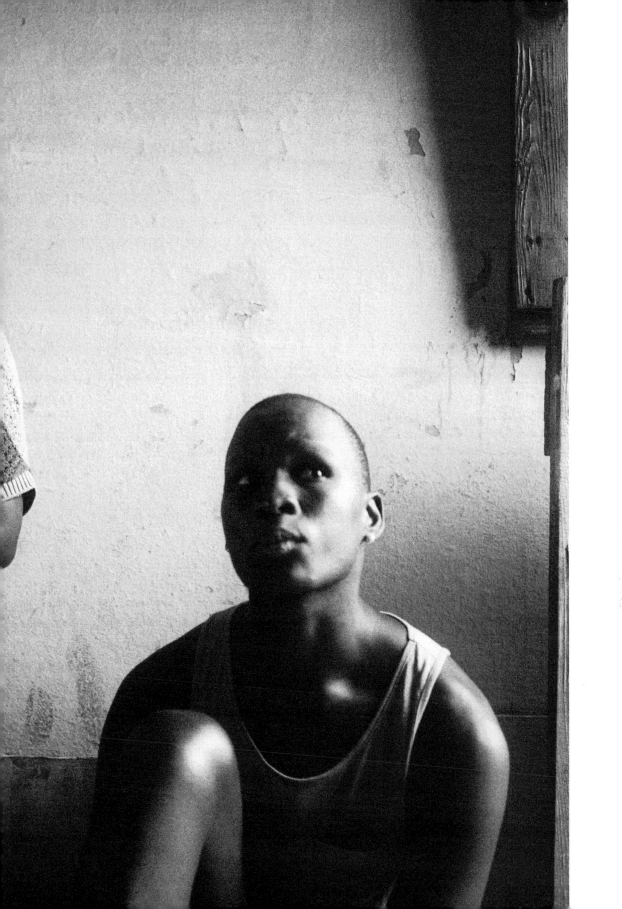

# THEY TREAT ME AS
# A MOTHER

# They Treat Me as a Mother
## MALWANDE (WANDY) ONCEYA
eQonce (KING WILLIAMSTOWN)

I remember that I told my mother in grade 1 that I cannot go to school trapped in a man's body. I told her "No, I'm not going to wear trousers." I was going to wear skirts and dresses. And my mum, she refused to buy me skirts and dresses, but my granny, she told my mother, "If he asks for it, you must buy those things." She is my best ally. She is still alive. She raised me.

When I decided to join my friends in the streets, I also started selling my body to get something to eat, to get money to pay for rent. It was very difficult. Sometimes the clients were beating us, beating us, beating us. But after a couple of months, they accepted us on the streets, and then they became our best customers. Once the business was doing well, I decided to leave school. I didn't see the point in going to school because I was getting money instead.

Then I got work with an HIV, TB and AIDS (HTA) organization because they came to us and gave me a job. HTA does prevention and outreach for people who are sex workers. I represent the sex workers there. I'm contributing condoms to the community, and also once a month, we do a sexual class to educate about health and why condoms are very important. The argument about the condom use is complicated because transgender people don't usually use condoms. We are arguing in the community about this. Someone says it's right to use condoms, someone says it's wrong; someone says, "I don't enjoy using when having sex."

## I am a woman
I go to the church. And I am wearing skirts in the church. They treat me as a mother. In church there is what we call mother's chairs and father's chairs, so I'm sitting on the mother's side even though they know I am gay. They accept me. I have never

had hormones. I would very much like to have hormones. I don't know how much they cost. I don't think there are any doctors here who would want to help us. It can be dangerous to talk about it, because people will beat you up. They will beat you to hell. I have seen it many times myself. It is as though I am trapped in this man's body. I am a woman, so I told them to please stop discriminating [against] us.

I also teach people about HIV and AIDS. At some point I got very ill. I couldn't walk, I was crawling. But little by little I got better, I just told myself that I must go out and tell people what this is, what my life is about, what life I am living; and I wish people could teach people, go to school and say, "Guys, you mustn't do this, you must not say these things." People usually respond positively when I try and educate them, they congratulate me. They say you do the right thing for the community. People are listening. I tell myself that I'm at least doing something good for the community. At least now more people accept me for who I am because I stand in front of them and tell them about my life, the whole story of my life. I had a relationship for two years. He was just really very, very nice, but he passed away. It was a car accident, and ever since, I haven't had another relationship.

## A woman, a mother

I would like to change my name to Priscilla. My mother was called Priscilla, my biological mother. That's why I like that name, because I don't know her. I got the feeling that if she was here, things would be better. At least I've got my granny next to me. She raised me. I told her, "Granny, I've got this and that, so I would love to just tell the whole family." And she is my friend. If I got a problem, I go to her.

I'm the one who's responsible. I'm staying with the kids. Make sure that they go to school. They are always eating. They are always clean. My mother went to work as a domestic sleep-in maid many years ago, so she wasn't around very much.

Sometimes she comes on a Friday and leaves late Sunday, then she goes back to work. That's the reason I am staying with the kids. I am the parent. I love this role. I love my children.

—April 2014

IN HER OWN WRITING

I was born in 1989 in Port Elizabeth. I grew up in King Williamtown. I knew that I was different from the age of six. How did I know I was different? I knew because I always identified with all things feminine. I had a fine upbringing. My mother is a single mother to four children. I am the second born, and we are two girls and two boys. I was raised in my mother's village of Leifveld, on the way to Alice, close to Tolofiyeni.

I cannot say that there was one night that we went to bed hungry. My mother worked and so did my grandmother. I have two uncles. We grew up in front of everyone in my mother's family. I think about those times with good memories. I was a girl who looked after everyone. I could never resonate with the tasks reserved for boys. I could see that this did not sit well with my uncle. People always ask mother why she raised me in such a feminine way. And the pressure; my mother left home because of the differences with my uncle. My mother got a room in another city. We went back home to the family village for the holidays and for the traditional events. When we went home, it was very tense. One day my family decided to have a meeting to find out why my mother had left the village. My mother explained that she was adamant about protecting me as a child. She made sure that we got everything we needed.

When they came home from school, I would look after everyone, make sure that their needs were fulfilled. Mother was a sleep-in maid somewhere in town, and it was my responsibility to look after the children. Girls taught me about life in the city. I started wandering around our neighborhood. I could come and go [as I] pleased. There was a day when I did not go

back home. That day was special to me. After school I was still
taking notes from the blackboard. I was waiting for my friend
Nomawhetu, when in came this other boy called Mphumzi.
He asked me why I was still at school. He was kind of annoy-
ing on such a hot day. He wanted to know who I was staying
with at home because he wanted to do homework with me. We
walked halfway home, me, him, and Nomawhetu when he said
he wanted to ask me something. I felt nervous wondering what
he wanted to say to me. I liked him, and I thought he might
like me too. The children were not due to be home until four,
so we would be alone. I made sandwiches with red jam. I sat
on the bed. Mphumzi walked over to close [the] door. I asked
why, but he just brushed me off. He walked over to the bed and
started kissing me. I got a hot flush, and it felt like everyone was
looking at us. He told me to get undressed, and I went along.
After all, I love this boy. His "totosa" was standing up straight!
He told me to lay on my tummy and the next thing I knew, I
felt something almost stabbing me. I jumped up. I complained
about it being painful. He was begging me to endure the pain.
He applied something, then it seemed somewhat better. We
used this lotion to enable penetration. I think it was painful
because I was so anxious. After it happened, there was almost an
awkward feeling when [we] tried talking to each other. At that
point I was just happy for him to leave. I had pain after the sex,
feeling almost frustrated. He was both exciting and painful for
me; there was a painful feeling, but I felt overjoyed at being a
woman. I didn't like him, and he confronted me about it. We
told my friends who took the red money from me. Nomawhetu
asked why I didn't report him to his parents, but that would
have been too awkward for me. I thought I would never have
sex again, but later I found some healing.

Xolani worked for the panel beaters not far from our house.
I always saw him passing by the house. I met Xolani at the
shop, and he asked me where I lived, so I gave him my address.
He said I must wait for him on the road. Once we reach [his]

place at Tsolo in Ginsberg, he lured me with this huge branch of fruits. I was disappointed to see the fruits. I thought he could have just brought it to my house. He switched on his Panasonic hi-fi, and soon enough Brenda Fassie's music blasted from the two small speakers. He offered to be my imaginary father. He picked me up and placed me on the bed. He even fed me the fruit. Little did I know that I would be my own imaginary mother. After the first few times I had been with him, I felt that I had everything. He gave me money, candy, and everything else I wish[ed] for. The day of the intimacy, he promised to take me somewhere else. In a funny moment, he put his arm around me and started kissing me. At first I protested, then went along with it. He put my hand on his penis, and it was the first time I saw an adult penis. The only penis I had ever seen was that of the boy I first had sex with, the small penis with the foreskin. I told him I could not take such a big penis, he just touched my body while jerking himself off. I thought what he did was good. I continued visiting him in Ginsberg, and it felt good because at that time, I felt like he was affirming my gender identity as a girl. The day he penetrated me . . . it was a weekday. I went to sleep at his place. He bought Coolee cool-drinks and Marie biscuits. The music was blasting from the speakers. Freddie Gwala's Amadamara played on the stereo. He played with me in a pleasurable way. We had now progressed from him just rubbing my anus to inserting his finger. I don't know what he used, but it was something slippery. I was riding him little by little, and the next moment he was inside me with just one jerk of his body. I gave one big scream. He asked me to persevere, and I did. I bled profusely afterward, but he took good care of me. He wiped my body. I told a lie when I got home. I said that I slept at Nomawhetu's house because I was not feeling well. I continued doing it with Xolani after my body healed. I slept with him three times. That was my introduction into womanhood.

—November 2015

THEY SEE ME NOW

PREVIOUS SPREAD: ZAZA OUTSIDE HER HOME IN DUNCAN VILLAGE THAT SHE CARES FOR

VERY MUCH. SHE LOVES GARDENING AND DECORATING. APRIL 2014

FOLLOWING SPREAD: ZAZA AND HER HUSBAND LIVE IN A ONE ROOM HOUSE IN DUNCAN

VILLAGE. HERE WITH THABISA (LEFT), APRIL 2014

# They See Me Now

ZAZA KWINANA

DUNCAN VILLAGE

The first time I realized who I am, I was wearing pants and I was going to school. I thought [to] myself, "No, I'm not comfortable." In my mind I have been a real woman ever since I was born. I was also playing with teddy bears and all the stuff with cooking. Some women, they are coming home and they fetch the rice, then they come to my home and pick the veggies. The other one is going to pick the meats that we will put on fires and cook over there. So that's when I first realized I'm a transgender.

[I told my mother,] she saw me when I was doing all of these things, so they have the debate, her and my father. She said [to him], "I see my son is feeling like a woman and almost all the time is playing with the women. So I don't think he is going to grow up as a man."

In my mind and inside, I feel like I'm a woman. When I went to the shop and bought sort of like Christmas clothes, [I said,] "Don't buy me trousers; buy me a short skirt and also pencil heels because I like to be high, the pencil heels." I was also singing, even to their location where I'm going to cook. So I came out to my family.

The neighbors, it was too difficult for them. [But because] my mother accept[ed] me and my father and my family, I don't care about the neighbors and all these people. In primary school, they didn't accept me. But as time went by, they see me, I'm a trans woman. I was wearing a dress for school and doing my hair nicely. I was singing a solo and choral music. But people don't understand. That's why I like [my work] spaces. We go to the schools and teach about transgender. I'm working with a sex worker program as I am a sex worker, too.

I like to be beautiful, and I want to buy my stuff like makeup and everything that I need in my house—grocery, pay

ZAZA AND HER HUSBAND HAVE BEEN MARRIED FOR EIGHT YEARS. DUNCAN VILLAGE, APRIL 2014

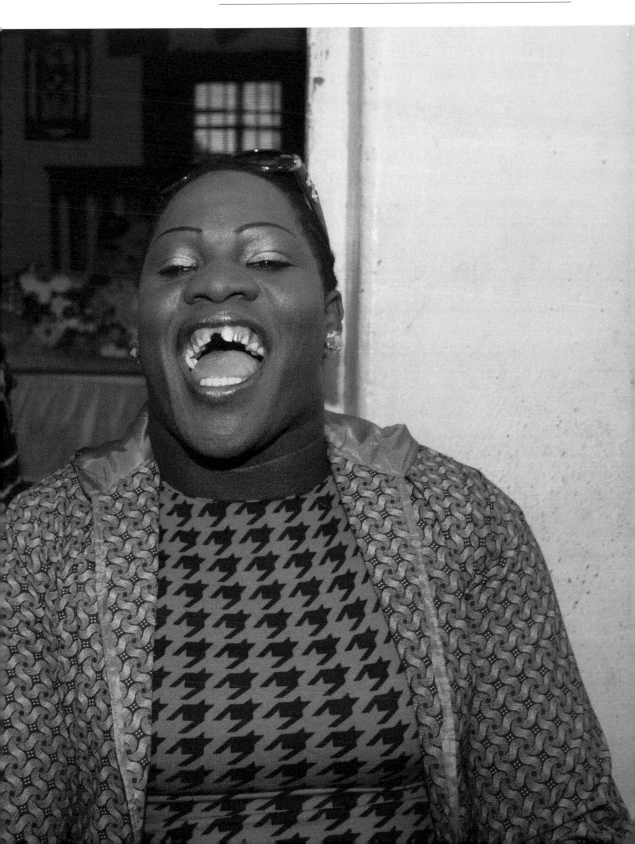

rent, pay everything. And also the furniture shop. So how can I get this money for the hormones? But I need the hormones.

It is around 250 rand per month for hormones. As I said, I've got many things to do. So this salary that I get, it's not enough to [cover] my needs. They said to us we can go to Gender Dynamix. They said to us they're going to provide us with the hormones, but it will take a long time. But we need the hormones right now.

[I left] school in eleventh grade. I wish I had gone more. [My] parents passed away. We have [other] relatives. They are not at all supportive of me. They don't feel angry. They [just] don't care.

I have not had circumcision. I feel like a woman, how can I go do the circumcision? Like I said, I'm a woman. If my husband heard I'm going to the circumcision, what would he think? He thinks I'm in between. So I would never do that. Instead of that, I can have a sex change.

We met in 2001. I was going to town. I went to town to enjoy myself. I see this guy and he's so . . . He said to me, "I love you." I said, "Okay." So we start to meet at the club, and have been together ever since. My mother-in-law loves me as well.

—April 2014

I have not had circumcision.

I feel like a woman,

how can I go do the circumcision?

Like I said, I'm a woman.

If my husband heard

I'm going to the circumcision,

what would he think?

ZAZA IS AN OUTREACH HIV OFFICER AND AIDS
ACTIVIST IN eMONTI

ZAZA ATTENDING ONE OF THE WEEKLY MEETINGS
FOR TRANSGENDER PEOPLE ON THE EASTERN
CAPE RUN BY S.H.E. eMONTI, APRIL 2014

IT'S A PAINFUL STORY

# Its a Painful Story
## SONWABISO (SOSO) MSELENI
TOILET CITY, EASTERN CAPE

My friend's name was Vuyisa. Ever since she was killed, we have had to live in fear in our community. We are wondering—who is next? We don't know who it was that killed her. My village, called Toilet City, may look quiet now, but at night, it's not. For trans women, it's not a safe place at all. Leigh Ann and her colleagues are giving us strength and motivate us, each and every day. If it wasn't for them, I think we wouldn't be able to stand up to the police. And we wouldn't be able to stand up to the communities that violate us as trans women. It's a painful story.

This murder has affected me badly. I thought that when you are being violated you could rely on the police in South Africa. Instead they, too, are violating trans women. It really hurts. I have tried to tell the police when they showed up at the South African National AIDS Council, that even when we have been violated, we cannot come to you because you are the first to discriminate [against] us. Some were interested to learn about this transgender thing because they only know about gays. Even gays have been violated by the police. People do not know the difference between trans and gays in South Africa, especially not in the townships.

## Circumcision
I haven't had any problems in my own family. If I want to wear makeup, I do, and they don't mind. That's what I like about my family. Even when I was a sex worker, they were there for me. I did tell them that I was working as a sex worker. I did have a choice. I saw sex work as a workplace for me. That is what I told them. So my family was very supportive of everything.

On my father's side, it was a little bit more of a problem. They are expecting me to marry a woman. They are expecting me to have a baby with another woman. My father was expecting me to have a circumcision. I did it because everyone agreed with my father on that. In fact, if I wanted to fit into society, I had to be circumcised. If I had refused, they would have chased after me, chased me away. It is different today, because today I could have explained to them that I am a trans woman. I would have sat them down and explained to them about my gender identity. But back in the day, I didn't know who I was. To be chased away from family leads most trans women into sex work. Most trans women and especially here in Toilet City, have been chased away by their families because they didn't want to be circumcised.

## Our work

We are trying to educate the police and our communities about transgender issues. I used to work for an organization in Cape Town, a sexual education and advocate's task force. In fact, I came there as an educator because I was a sex worker. I would head our movement with other sex workers and educate sex workers about health and HIV and the use of condoms. I later became a site coordinator, then a provincial coordinator. Then I ended the work because the program was on hold because of financial problems. Now I'm just staying in my home. I'm not working.

—April 2014

SOSO AT S.H.E.'S OFFICES IN

eMONTI THE FIRST TIME WE MET

HER IN APRIL 2014

"THIS IS WHAT A SEX WORKER LOOKS LIKE." SOSO OUTSIDE HER HOME IN TOILET CITY. EMONTI, NOVEMBER 2015

SOSO AT HOME IN TOILET CITY, NOVEMBER 2015: "I USED TO HAVE A JOB, AND I COULD BUY THE FURNITURE FOR MY FAMILY THAT YOU SEE HERE IN MY HOME."

AMASIKO; IT'S TRADITION

# Amasiko; It's Tradition

## THABISA MOYIKWA

DUNCAN VILLAGE, EASTERN CAPE

I don't have feelings for girls. I have feelings for guys. But my
parents didn't know that. At the age of eighteen, I went to Cape
Town. I stayed two years in Cape Town. My parents called
me, and they said I must come back to East London. I start
telling my parents, "You know what? I'm attracted to another
man." My father said, "I knew it from the start that you were
not going to be dating girls." He didn't have a problem with
it. And my mother too doesn't have a problem. My parents
both love me for who I am, so I decided to come out to all the
people, and then I started dating guys openly. I can tell anyone
that I am a trans woman and I like sleeping with other guys. If
someone asks me why, I tell them that it's the feeling that I feel
inside. I grew up being like this. [If people] label me, [I say,]
"You're full of yourself because when you do something, you do
it for yourself." Everyone has his own issues. So I told myself
that this is me.

Not many people here accept you for who you are. They
were those people who said, "No, this is disgusting." And there's
others who say, "No, this is her choice. If she likes doing this,
she must do it."

My principal at [the] high school, he didn't like me at all. I
say, "This is where I belong. This is the school that the government built for us to learn." He was my teacher for my subject. I
liked history. He would come and say, "Get out of my class." I
would say, "Why?" He said, "You can't wear earrings here." I
would take off the earrings and then come in and say, "I took
them off." Then he would say, "Why—who are you?" And I
would say, "No sir, I'm just a human like others." And he would
say, "No, man. You're a mofee," or he would call me names
in front of the pupils at school. They would laugh and I'd be
heartbroken. He would say before the test, before I write the

THABISA SHARES HER HOME WITH
SEVERAL FAMILY MEMBERS INCLUDING
HER COUSIN AND HER COUSIN'S
KIDS. THABISA'S COUSIN SUFFERS FROM
TB. DUNCAN VILLAGE, APRIL 2014

THABISA (RIGHT) EXPLAINS HOW DIF-
FICULT IT IS TO SHARE SUCH A SMALL
ROOM WITH SO MANY FAMILY MEM-
BERS. HER NAMESAKE TWIN THABISA
(LEFT) PASSED AWAY FROM AIDS-
RELATED ILLNESSES A FEW MONTHS
AFTER THIS PHOTO WAS TAKEN.
DUNCAN VILLAGE, APRIL 2014

test, he would say, "You failed. Even if you write the test and if you don't write the test, you fail." It was the most challenge I've ever had.

I like communicating with the people. I'm an outreach volunteer. We go to places, distribute condoms. We do an outreach once a week. I don't have anything. I don't have money. I'm broke. So at least when I'm here, I don't think that I'm broke. I just stay and have some tea, and then they find some food and then I eat it, and when I go home, I get to watch TV. I like it. I like what I'm doing there.

Those who do hormones or eat hormones are those who have money, mostly. So if you don't have money, you don't have [hormones]. You can be whatever you want to be, just a trans woman like me. I'm not dressing to impress. I'm dressing the way I used to dress. I don't have to wear a dress to show that I'm a trans woman. I don't have to wear things that make me a girl because if anyone wants to see, they can see when I walk up the street. I don't walk like a guy. I walk like a girl because I'm a girl. You can see me when I'm walking, I'm walking like I'm walking. Then people will notice that, "Hey, this is a girl. She's a girl."

## Amasiko

It was 2006, on June 16. My father told me that when I finish exams, I'll be going to the Mountain. I said, "Okay, that's fine. I'll do it." They gave me the money to buy a bottle of brandy so that you will celebrate, they finish it, what they're doing to you. There were many. Maybe six, seven. I went there and then they come and surrounded me. I was lost, and then I saw all the friends of mine. My schoolmates were there and my age group. I said, "Oh my God. I mustn't show that I'm a coward. I must be this person—make myself strong and then they're done."

They're using a knife. It's used for everyone. Two sides are sharp. It's a long knife. I was scared but to be scared of something that you don't know if . . . They can spread HIV with the knife. It can happen—it can spread.

I felt dizzy after. And then I woke up. I [had to stay] there
a month. In the Bush, in the Mountain. They build you a
hut. And then they always tell me that everything's going to be
fine. Stay calm and you're going to do well. You have to eat a
starch with no water. Can't drink water. We have many cultures. Others don't go to the Mountain. They just do it around
the house. Amasiko. [Meaning] it's tradition. So it depends on
how you do your tradition. All the blacks doing it. I'm Xhosa—
Xhosa has to go this way. I'm twenty-five.

[Before it happened,] people said, "No, he's not going to
stand that pain." And then I tell myself, "You have to be strong
for them to make sure that I prove them wrong." "Thabo's a
mofee? He can't stand the pain on the Mountain." I got out
on the twenty-seventh of July. Friends of mine went to the
Mountain together, and I started dating one of them. I'm in a
relationship with someone I went to the Bush with. [I was in]
a relationship with [another] guy. He was shot while he was
robbing. All my friends who went to the Bush became thugs.
That's why my mother and my father loved me because I never
do such a thing. They always love me, and they say, "Oh my
baby, thanks to God you [are] who you are today because if you
are this way, you're maybe attacked and maybe you are dead a
long time ago." I'm always with girls because I don't like fights
and other things.

I'm a trans. I know that because the things that I think
inside [are] the female things. I clean at home. I cook. I also
knit. I do other things that girls do, and I always party with
girls, and I'm always surrounded by girls and they like me. I
always make them laugh. I can make them laugh too much. My
name means happiness.

*Ubuntu*. When talking about *Ubuntu*, to give to. I'm struggling to get a phone. My friend has a second phone and says,
"My friend, use this phone so that I can get hold of you or reach
you." We call that *Ubuntu*, or if that guy or that lady down
there—I saw a lady [with] too many packages and then I say,

People were calling us

like two birds,

the two birds that are made

for peace.

They told us that we

used to fly

when we were around,

making peace.

They saw two birds.

Now she's dead.

THABISA WITH HER MOTHER WHO WORKS AS A LIVE-IN MAID AND IS SELDOM AT HOME. DUNCAN VILLAGE, APRIL 2014

"May I carry your packets?" That is also *Ubuntu*, when a person is doing something for another person.

## "No one will rape a boy"

I've not experienced rape. I've never been raped. Some nights at the club, there would be these guys buying people booze and then say, "Let's go to sleep," and if you don't, they will beat you up and then they'll take you and sleep with you whether you want or not. That is rape. If I said, "No, I don't want it now. Maybe some other time." That's rape. And then in the summer, my boyfriend, he would ask to do sex with him. If I don't want, I don't want because that's me. He said, "You're not going to go outside, and I'm going to beat you up until you give me sex." I go, "No, I don't want to give you sex because I'm tired. We've been doing this all week." Then you beat me up and then you do sex, that's a rape.

But if you go to the police, they will say, "What happened?" And I will say, "That guy raped me." "That guy raped you? Who are you? What are you? Are you a lady or a boy or a girl? What are you?" And I will say, "I'm trans." "Hey, no one will rape you here. No one will rape a boy. What are you thinking? You're not a girl. You have not been raped." They don't know that these things happen. A guy can be raped. The police, they would say also, "You deserve it because you wanted to be raped." So justice here is not working at all.

The newspaper does not work to our advantage. They won't say a man has been raped by another man. Never. But there is another thing, if the police doesn't know that, they will say it's just a scoop, so it's nothing. They're taking it lightly. They never write anything about [LGBT]. There's no education in this place. No education at all.

—April 2014

NOVEMBER 2015

Since April 2014 I've been doing outreach for Social, Health
and Empowerment (S.H.E.), testing people, educating people
about HIV and AIDS, and about being transgender. Most
people don't know what transgender is. They know only gay
and lesbian. I am educating people in my community. There is
a stigma when it comes to transgender. There is a lot of violence
toward transgender people. I want to try and fix that so that it
might not happen to trans like it happened to me. I was almost
raped by a guy who was always teasing me about being the
person I am. He was making fun of me in front of people and
always punched me when he saw me. He touched me, and I
didn't like it.

But it happened the other day. I was drunk, he took advantage of me. He slapped me, first my face, and then when I saw
blood, my nose was bleeding, he kicks me. After I tried to fight
him, he choked me, and I ran out of air. I couldn't breathe. It
was painful. It was really, really hurtful. I had to cry, but I didn't
know how to; I didn't have a breath to cry with, because he
was choking me. I had to find a way to get out of his hands. I
tried to make a sound, banging on the wall so that the neighbor
could hear me, which was where his older brother was staying.
After I made more noise, his older brother came in and stopped
him. But he shouted, saying that he arrived at his place and had
found me naked. And I said, "No, you are lying." And then the
brother backed me and said, "No, I heard your conversation.
Don't lie and say that he was naked when you came here."

I went to the police with my friends and my mum. The
police said I must go to the hospital. When I arrived at the
hospital, I had injured on my hand where he had stabbed me
with a screwdriver. He stabbed me in the hand and then he
beat me up, and I was bruised in the face. It took a long time
to go to hospital and then to come back to the police station
afterward. I was just so tired. It is dangerous to go to the police.

PREVIOUS SPRREAD: THABISA WITH HER MANY
COUSINS AND NEIGHBORS. DUNCAN VILLAGE,
APRIL 2014

AFTER HER SISTER'S DEATH, THABISA MOVED INTO HER OWN PAD. "EVERY MORNING I GO AND FETCH WATER, THEN HAVE A BATH, GET DRESSED, CLEAN CLOTHES AND GO TO WORK." THABISA SHOWS US PHOTOS OF HERSELF IN A YELLOW SILK GOWN. SHE WON THE TITLE "1ST PRINCESS" AT THE EASTERN CAPE MISS TRANS DIVA PAGEANT. DUNCAN VILLAGE, NOVEMBER 2015

It's dangerous because he will come after me and say "Drop the case or else;" maybe he will kill me. The day after, I had to go with the police to the place where the attacker lived. The police took him to the police station. But then the morning after, I saw him coming through my front door. After that, I was afraid of going out because I didn't know what he would do to me. I had to be strong so that I could go out. I went back to the police and asked them why they had let him out. They said they let him go because they didn't take it so seriously. A few days later I went back to the police with my friend to confront the police, but the police just laughed at me. The police didn't even give me warning that they were releasing him. They didn't give me a letter. So I prayed that God would know what to do. Then later I learned that this guy had died. He got stabbed and shot. He was doing the same thing to other people.

I have many siblings, my sisters and my cousins, girls mostly. When I go out, I'm always around girls. I would fight with them to play the mother because I like to be a mother. I wear high heels sometimes. I didn't tell myself that I was different because people just said I was a guy who liked to wear girl things. I was the age of six. I went to school, and people began to notice me. My voice was girly. I sounded like a girl and I walked like a girl.

Sometimes I wore skirts. Sometimes they laughed at my silly stuff. I like when they were laughing. Those who didn't like me, they didn't want to play with me. But I would always have someone who loved to be with me, and it would usually be a girl. Our surroundings are very traditional. So in this type of culture, trans don't feel comfortable coming out because if you come out here, you will get stigma. You will get criticized by people and sometimes beaten. Some will say, "Why are you acting like a 'mofee'?"

Then they will slap you because of who you are. I'll try to teach people about the way I feel, and then I'll tell him or her that this is my life. I live the way I want to and because my family accepts me for who I am. That's what I always tell every-one else.

Since you were last here, my cousin Thabisa has died. It really, really breaks my heart because she was like my twin sister. I loved her too much. People were calling us like two birds, the two birds that are made for peace. They told us that we used to fly when we were around, making peace. They saw two birds. Now she's dead. I moved to my own place after that. I need my privacy. Because we have older brothers who tell others what to do and what not to do. I don't want to have someone telling me that. I do what I like. That's why I'm living here. And with my friend around, it's all good because she treats me like a queen. When I'm at work she will clean the house and wash my clothes. She will cook, she will do everything.

I'd like to take hormones, but people I've seen say they develop big stomachs and they will have those side effects like they get shy around other people. And they get depressed as well. This medication is not good for me. I don't like sleeping. I like to be around people. I like to sleep at night.

What makes me feel like a woman is when I'm around other ladies, chatting about stuff. Most ladies speak about their periods. I don't have periods. But I speak like I have my period. "I have my period too!" Then we speak about partners and boys. Being massaged by a guy, ah, it makes me feel more like a woman. Every morning I go and fetch water, then have a bath, get dressed, clean clothes, and go to work. It used to be safe to walk through Duncan Village early in the morning, but now it is getting more dangerous.

—November 2015

THABISA (LEFT) AND PHIWE (RIGHT) NEAR A FIRE THAT BROKE OUT IN NOVEMBER 2015.
FIRES ARE A COMMON DESTINY FOR THE TIN ROOF HOMES IN DUNCAN VILLAGE

PREVIOUS SPREAD: THABISA WITH HER EXTENDED FAMILY. DUNCAN VILLAGE, APRIL 2014

ALL THE DREAMS THAT

I HAVE

# All The Dreams That I Have
## FIKILE

DUNCAN VILLAGE, EASTERN CAPE

My name is Fikile. I am thirty-one years old. I live in Duncan
Village. I think I was about six when I knew I was a girl. I live
with my mother, sister, and two brothers. My father is not living
with us. I'm suffering. Sometimes I don't have anything to eat.
People don't treat me nice. I've got support from one other girl.
Duncan Village is a poor place. I would like to go very far away.
Maybe even to another country.

I'm not scared, but I'm not feeling good at all. I became HIV
positive in 2004.

I am thinking about a lot of things. All the dreams that I
have. Sometimes when I do "business," the men force me to
do things to me. Sometimes they will give me the money, but
sometimes they don't want to give me the money first; they
would go about and do their business, and sometimes they like
making me cross; and after I have given them what they want,
they beat me up after sex. Sometimes they beat me before we
have sex. Sometimes they don't pay.

My good memories are when I was a child and going out
with my friends to the shops to buy something nice to eat.
Maybe see animal[s] in the water, taking a walk, maybe go and
visit friends.

My family, they treat me sometimes like I am not a human
being. They treat me like an animal. They mess with my mind
and they want to fight. My family does not belong to any
church. I'll be free when I can love my life as a woman. Then I
will be free.

—April 2014

FIKILE SAID EVEN THOUGH IT WAS HARD FOR HER TO TELL US HER STORY, SHE WANTS HER STORY TOLD. EMONTI, APRIL 2014

# Lifting Spirits

BY HERB SCHREIER

MARCH, 2017

As I sat down to write this from my cocoon in Berkeley, California, a city whose politics goes from liberal to progressive to radical but never to the conservative brand of Republicanism, I looked for any bright moment to bring me out of the depression I had sunk into the night the election was lost. That Donald Trump would rule sent me into a tailspin to the point that now, two months later, I was still having trouble reading the news section of the *New York Times*.

I was present for the so-called second wave of feminism—the women's symbolic "burning of the bras," the equivalent of men burning their draft cards; and Muhammad Ali being sent to jail for refusing to fight the "white man's war against the yellow man" in Vietnam. The civil rights movement has made many gains and taken many turns, some peaceful and some not; the Black Power movement, for example, showed just how far a government in a democracy could violate its own constitution. All these movements did move the cultural wars forward, and some of the gains are now taken for granted: women came out of the kitchen and nursery to go to work, black women and men went to college and to good-paying jobs, abortion rights became the law of the land. And now we are faced with the ugly reality of a President and a Congress who will try to move us all backward to a very dark age indeed.

Writing this, I am reminded of how this book came to be. Kris and I were presenting at a trans-health conference in Bangkok, where we met Leigh Ann van der Merwe, who told us of her work in South Africa and invited us to document her community. We headed first to a pan-African trans advocacy conference in Nairobi, Kenya, before we went to South Africa.

The purpose of the conference in Kenya, sharing strategies for resisting the poor treatment of LGBT people from all over

Africa, had to be disguised, as were the names of the partici-
pants, since most of them were "illegal" in their African home
countries. Being gay (and trans) is against the law in thirty-six
countries, and in four it can lead to a death sentence.

From our landing in Johannesburg, we took a short flight,
passing over the birthplace village of Nelson Mandela, and
landed in East London in April 2014. I had been to South Africa
some years before, at the beginning of the end of Apartheid.
Mandela had been released, and the country was preparing
for its first election involving all of its people. Travel was now
encouraged to the boycotted country, and I remembered a trip
to the Kruger game park, where black people had not been
allowed unless they were to be at the somewhat dangerous head
of a group trekking on foot to see the animals—lions, hippos,
and rhinos if you were lucky. One of Mandela's first steps was
to take thousands of South African black children to see their
birthright.

What had become of post-Apartheid South Africa? Kris and
I wondered. On our second visit in 2015 we found it difficult to
ignore the townships, Soweto looking much like what we had
seen in the movies of early struggles in Cape Town. Difficult as
well were the news reports of Jacob Zuma, the reelected president
now in his second term, a polygamist who had been tried for
rape and was building a mansion costing some twenty-two mil-
lion rand. Taxi drivers, aware that we were tourists, continued to
proudly tout the story of the first heart transplant the world had
known, pointing out the hospital in Cape Town where Christiaan
Barnard accomplished it. It happened several times on my first
trip there, and now I recalled that on that trip in the 1990s, half
of the infants on a ward I visited at the Red Cross Hospital were
HIV infected and whose mothers could not talk about it when
they returned home. Later I and the rest of the world read with
horror that the second ANC president, Thabo Mbeki, denied
for years that there was such a thing as AIDS and that now many
thousands of South Africans were paying the price.

Fortunately we had our guide, Thabisa, from S.H.E,, who worked as a volunteer for outreach projects. She became our translator of Xhosa, as well as a living encyclopedia of who and what the townships were all about. From our hours in the car and out walking with her in the townships, and especially being invited into people's abodes, a condition Kris lobbied for, to be able to take her photographs and write about what she saw, I could, as a pediatrician and child psychiatrist, begin to absorb a picture of life in one of the largest townships in South Africa.

Thabisa, who quickly bonded with Kris from the time we met on our first trip, was indispensable. Kris, more intrepid than I, and less reserved, threw herself into the work with enthusiasm and reverence for the people of Ama Xhosa. She starts from a point of view, rare in my profession, that you have to meet people where they are . . . in their neighborhood and in their homes, if they will let you. Thabisa was at one with this and was comfortable taking us out to meet the people who had agreed to talk with us, many welcoming us into their homes.

Kris, the photojournalist with a Rolleiflex and a video camera around her neck, and I, a bit older and "the doctor," were treated with respect wherever we went.

Two images from our trips to South Africa remain chiseled in my mind:

Thabisa wanted us to meet her family. After driving out to Duncan Village, up on a hill, we got a bird's-eye view of the homes, familiar to anyone who has seen movies showing the townships: many small shacks of corrugated metal, most without running water and few with toilets, and dirt roads. There is slow progress, with a few people granted small parcels of land to own, who build multiple-room dwellings, mainly of cinder block, some with running water. Far off in the distance we saw the skyline of East London which could be that of a medium-sized city anywhere in the world. On our second day there, we found ourselves in the small one-room abode that Thabisa called home, crowded with three generations of her family, a dozen or so people.

While chatting away, Kris eagerly taking loads of pictures, Thabisa introduced me to her "sister," a cousin, a beautiful woman in her twenties, and asked if I could look at a wound under her headdress that had festered for some time. I long ago learned that my being introduced as a child psychiatrist didn't stop people from seeking out medical advice or exempt me from giving it, and I agreed. She unwrapped the scarf from her head to reveal a large, bulging pus-filled scalp abscess. One glance substantiated the seriousness of what I was seeing. I asked about the availability of antibiotics; they had been ineffective. Had she been cleaning the wound well? She did, but the conditions were so bad and at that point hardly beneficial. Shortly after that, with what I hoped was a disguised worried look and a wan smile to her cousin, I took Thabisa aside and asked in a whisper whether her cousin had been tested for HIV (South Africa has the largest percentage of any population in Africa of people infected with HIV). She had, and was found to be positive for HIV. Knowing the resistance in the country for such a long time to recognize the very existence of HIV/AIDS, I asked, with Thabisa translating for me, whether she was being treated for it. She was, and then I was taken aback to find out that she was not taking the prescribed HIV medications. It turned out that she could not handle the known side effect of the antiviral medications she was given, saying that it was destroying her stomach, and she couldn't take the pills with food as prescribed, because she couldn't afford to buy food!

As a doctor, either you are schooled by experience into resignation or hopelessness, or you demand that a preventable situation, such as the one here, be rectified. I have always tried the latter but have often been discouraged by the all-too-frequent failure to achieve what was possible in the face of some bureaucratic rule or logjam, or just a shoulder-shrug callousness. After we left the family, we visited the government's ruling party African National Congress representative in the area and were told that he was not in and was not expected. We later learned that he earned a salary of $2,700 a month, an astonishing sum by the standards of the townships. I wrote a letter to this ombudsperson as soon as I returned to the States so that I could send it on hospital stationery. In the letter, I introduced myself as a supporter of the boycott of South Africa, which we felt had some effect on ending Apartheid and the release of Nelson Mandela. I also said that I once knew Harold Volpe, a white exiled South African ANC member who had organized the education plan for the South African children at the end of Apartheid. In the Cape Town museum, there is a picture of Harold with other members of the ANC. Indeed, I found myself thinking about him (he died at age 59 from overwork and a bad heart in the middle of the education development process) when Kris and I found ourselves on the streets in the townships and in East London at a time when school let out, surrounded by grade school and high school children in clean and pressed uniforms representing many different schools, playfully walking on their way home.

I wrote to the ombudsperson, perplexed by the lack of the availability of food for Thabisa's cousin, and how important it was for her treatment. Her husband had one day packed up and left her and their children. As expected, nothing came of the letter, and we learned to our sadness a few months later that Thabisa's cousin had died and that the family was taking care of her young children.

Near the end of our second trip, which took us now farther afield to meet transwomen, we told Thabisa that we would like to cook a meal for her and her family. She was delighted, and we set off to shop for food. She guided us to a market, a small shop on the outskirts of the township. We let her pick the menu. As we packed our eighth or ninth wrapped, double platter of thin, pretty, fatty pork chops, I wondered out loud how many relatives she was expecting, and she said that she had invited a few friends as well. It was Sunday and no alcohol could be sold, so the liquid refreshments were limited to sodas and juices. As we

PHIWE (RIGHT) INVITED US TO PHOTOGRAPH HER IN HER HOME IN DUNCAN VILLAGE, NOVEMBER 2015

gathered the food together and paid for it, I asked her about getting some ice cream for dessert and was told that there was no freezer. I began to think about what else might be missing and why I had not remembered the limited amenities, nay essentials, of the house we had been to. It was dusk when we entered a small, low-ceilinged, corrugated-metal house with a tiny kitchen and one electric outlet for the electric fry pan, the hot plate to boil water for the corn, and the small fridge.

The room next to the kitchen, a fair-sized living room, was lively with little kids and young adult women, close friends of Thabisa united in the moment's festiveness. Kris looked right at home and was welcomed into the ample bosom of Thabisa's cousin, who clearly did not want her to leave, but knew that I would need help preparing the food. This cousin clearly got my New York humor, and we managed in a very simpatico vein to turn out plates of pork chops after I got over my disappointment at not being able to serve the meal I had envisioned. We had to take turns keeping up with the demand for the pork chops and getting the water hot enough to cook some of the corn. As the music grew louder, other friends and family showed up, and only later on did a few men drift in. The kids were clearly enjoying their meal and sat on the floor playing boisterously and laughing a lot, no one trying to hush them up. They let out a shriek when Thabisa brought out and opened the several boxes of cookies that we had bought.

What started with me bemoaning the stripped-down meal turned into a sense of enjoyment and memories of the long-ago block parties when I was a kid in my Italian and Jewish Bronx neighborhood. I now had yet another bodily sensation to go with the wonderful phrase *Ubuntu* that we had been experiencing in our work. *Ubuntu* was something that came up over and over as we worked our way through the extreme class differences we saw on our trip from Cape Town, driving through beautiful, lush flower and game parks up the east coast of South Africa. Farther up the cape, as we passed through Port Elizabeth, the towns were a mixture of unemployed or very poorly employed black people surrounded by gated neighborhoods in the architectural style of the Afrikaaners; and finally to East London, with a similar inner-city population, scraping by, surrounded by more gentrified gated homes on the outskirts. There were two gorgeous beaches facing the Indian Ocean, the one in town we were warned about not going to for safety reasons, and the other one populated almost completely by white families and groups of children on various sports or boating outings. East London was to be our home base, starting out from the S.H.E. offices.

Phiwe's story is also memorable for me, one that gives me hope in the face of my work at a hospital in a poorer part of Oakland, California, working with traumatized youth and young transgender people, some only three or four years old, coming in with their parents, demanding to be heard that they are not the person that their biological bodies would indicate. Phiwe's story speaks of profound physical and psychological trauma, but she, like so many we met on these trips, has found a way to resist the slings and arrows of daily life for gender-variant people. She spends time educating and advocating, not just for the communities, but at conferences across the continent of Africa and beyond, amid deep-seated mistrust, dislike, and hatred of people who dare to challenge the "natural" order of things, that of just a "man or woman." S.H.E. has given a voice for transwomen as well as other LGBT people to voice their humanity in a way enriching us all, for when we accept difference, we are all better off.

For me, my most endearing and enduring moment occurred when we were at Phiwe's home to interview her, a tall, lean, strikingly beautiful woman who also worked at S.H.E. We found ourselves outside on a typical dusty street of Duncan Village, approached by the usual crowd of little ones, shy at first, then bolder, pointing at the cameras, laughing, and making fun as they surrounded us. Suddenly a little boy came running through the crowd and wrapped himself around Phiwe's legs,

with a big smile and a shout. Phiwe explained that he was one
of two possible transgender children she knew.

I had my camera out and began shooting photos, which
always drew a larger crowd of kids who came running to get
in the picture. We went to where Phiwe lived, a corrugated,
galvanized tin shed with a hard linoleum floor. Her little friend
had followed. I asked about him, of course, and was told that
he is teased mercilessly as he is quite effeminate, something I
had noticed as well, and that his mother is at her wits' end to
know what to do with and for him. He is called Mophi, a name
used the way "fag" was used in the primary schoolyards of the
south Bronx where I grew up, and which took me some time to
understand stood for gay, and then quite some time longer to
get what that meant.

I asked Phiwe to see if the boy's mother might want to
come and talk about what her concerns were, and Phiwe left
and came back minutes later with his mom. We spoke through
translations, having sent the little boy to the street to play,
which he did without apparent suspicion or trepidation. And
the heartrending story I am so familiar with from my practice
came pouring out of mom: how she loved her little boy; how
she felt she couldn't protect him from the slights of the street
from both young and old; how she was afraid for him; and how
she wanted to know, could she protect him growing up and if
there was any cure.

She listened with genuine interest to the usual talk I would
give in Oakland to parents who came in with a sensitive little
boy who was effeminate and teased and treated not only by
the kids in the community, but by relatives, as if there were
something drastically wrong with him. And I told her two
possibilities for the future, and that increasingly in South Africa,
people like Phiwe were working to organize against the assaults
on perfectly normal little kids like hers. I mentioned that we
had dropped off several books for the new S.H.E. clinic's library,
one by a colleague, Dr. Diane Ehrensaft, *The Gender Creative*

*Child*; that she could have some help getting it read to her in translation (Phiwe volunteered immediately); and that I could be reached at any time for questions. One thing I shared with her was that children such as her son, maybe daughter, in my experience, are more creative, having, from an early age, to deal with difference; and with support, often they come through it and are in many ways better off than the rest of us who take our early development for granted without asking these profoundly interesting questions.

But now, more than when I first started this essay upon returning from South Africa, I feel the importance of this trip, and a need to recall and revisit it: the spirit and exuberance of the children and the families in the street and in their homes; the pride and welcoming grace with which they accepted us and invited us into their homes; the political movements, such as S.H.E., that drive a project now underway to test people for HIV and tuberculosis while they are still treatable, and set out to educate at all levels. I needed this reflection on the struggles of these people—because with the election of a narcissistic, out-of-control womanizer with so little grace to lead the richest and most powerful nation in the world, I had experienced a need to resign. I was on the front lines of the battles of the 1970s and 1980s, and though there was still a ways to go yet, there was a belief in my cohort of activists that slow and upward progress toward human rights and dignity could be achieved. It was hard work with many, many setbacks. And then at the speed of a bolt of lightning, I was amazed at just how easily this country and nations all around the world could slip back so rapidly into the conditions that brought hunger, disease, death, and destruction to so many, seemingly without remorse and a sense of righteousness in the cause of returning to the evils of the past. I found myself leaning on the spirit and resiliency of the people of the Eastern Cape, and I resolved to pick up the placards once again and renew the fight and march again against inequality, not only out in the world but here in our own backyard.

# TULIE NAOMI VILI

# A EULOGY

# An Angel and a Queen for the People

BY RONNIE TYAKUMA

NOVEMBER 2, 2016

Tulie . . . a friend, sister, and child with a lot of dreams and a heart of gold. She was Passionate, Brave, Smart, and Funny. She wanted more in life and had given a lot to get where she was.

Ever since I knew Tulie before she got into activism for transgender people, her first love in this world was modeling. In the East London–Mdantsane area when you said modeling, you couldn't say it without her name. She was well known for always being in the spotlight, wearing her form-fitting, tight dresses, and for making people feel like Kings and Queens. When she walked in the streets, on the stage, and I swear, even in her dreams, she was strutting like the world's eyes are all on her. Her gold heart was full of love, peace, and joy, and that showed from how she treated all the people, and you could see it in her smile and eyes. She never wanted to see anyone depressed or sad. You would fight with Tulie, but seconds later, she wants peace and wants to laugh about what happened. She was starting up her own agency for all the school kids who also wanted to do modeling; we settled on the name "Modeling Agency & Youth Development." She wanted to share her dreams and passion with the rest of the world. She was building her own Empire at her own pace and in her spare time.

She was an office assistant at Social, Health, and Empowerment. And she was assisting in all the programs of the organization. She never slack[ed] or questioned the duties she was given; she always held her head up and worked. Any differences she had at work, she let slide; and at other times, she would share them with her friend when she got off work. She was very passionate about making sure all transgender people knew their rights and were respected and treated as humans. She would join the team when it came to Transgender People sensitization

RONNIE TYAKUMA AND TULIE NAOMI VILI OUTSIDE TULIE'S HOME IN NOVEMBER 2015. TULIE PASSED AWAY FROM MULTIDRUG-RESISTANT TUBERCULOSIS ONLY 10 MONTHS AFTER THIS PHOTO WAS TAKEN. MDANTSANE, NOVEMBER 2015

I started working at Social, Health,

and Empowerment after I won

Ms. Trans Diva in September 2014.

As winner of Ms. Trans, you have to do your duties

as the reigning queen,

going out and helping the trans community.

My friend told me

there was a competition that she thought

I might be interested in,

so I entered the competition

and I saw people there just like me.

People who were transgender;

people who were free;

people who lived their life

according to what they wanted.

—Tulie, November 2015

TULIE SHARED WITH US SOME OF THE PHOTOS ON HER BEDROOM WALL OF HER WINNING THE
TRANS DIVA PAGEANT. MDANTSANE, NOVEMBER 2015

TULIE NAOMI VILI

TULIE AND HER BROTHER IN THEIR FAMILY KITCHEN. MDANTSANE, NOVEMBER 2015

and always wanted people to look up to her. She would share all her personal stories to encourage young trans women not to give up or feel inferior.

If her purpose in life was to make people happy, then she accomplished that.

She fell ill at the office and had difficulty breathing. Later on, the doctors diagnosed her with Multidrug-resistant tuberculosis (MDR-TB). Her mother had shared that [Tulie] once nursed an MDR patient years ago, but she never checked for TB herself. She was hospitalized for a few months, and then, sadly, she passed on.

# BE WHO YOU ARE

# Be Who You Are

NCESHI VENA

KWANOBUHLE, ETINARHA (UITENHAGE)

I am Nceshi Ncamile Vena. I was born a boy, but I am transgender. I used to label myself as gay, a drag queen, because I wore women's clothing. I grew up in Kwanobuhle, Uitenhage. I started living here in the Peace Village when I was eighteen years old. I first stayed with my brother, who is mentally ill. The people in this area do not have a problem with me because I am just being myself. They embrace me for who I am, which is very important, to be just who you are and for people to love you the way you are.

My father had a problem with me as I was growing up. I never knew anything about transgender until I met Phiwe in November 2014 in Port Elisabeth. People like her and Leigh Ann made me who I am today. I now know that I am trans and that I am a woman. I am a strong woman. My mother was the one who supported me. I love her so much. She had a stroke. She is now very sick. My father has finally accepted me and my sexuality.

When I was going to be circumcised, it was not that I wanted to go to the Bush and initation school. I knew I was a woman, and I did not want to go, but I had to please my father and his family. It is customary to go to the Bush.

I love my community because they have accepted me. Whenever there is a traditional ceremony, they know I do not mix with the males; they know I am always with the women and that I wear a skirt. I am a very well-known person around here. Not everyone is supportive of me, maybe eighty percent of the people here. The rest do not approve of the fact that I am hanging out with females. The majority of my community members love me and embrace me for who I am. I am so very proud of being transgender.

That is why I say: be who you are, don't compromise, because people will love you for who you are.

—November 2015

NCESHI VENA AT HOME IN PEACE VILLAGE, NOVEMBER 2015

PREVIOUS SPREAD: NCESHI TOLD US HER STORY IN HER FIRST LANGUAGE, ISIXHOSA. SHE

FEELS SAFE LIVING IN PEACE VILLAGE. NOVEMBER 2015

NCESHI ON HER WAY HOME FROM WORK IN PEACE VILLAGE. NOVEMBER 2015

I WANT TO BE LOVED

# I Want To Be Loved

## THANDILE FANGA

HAALANI LOCATION, eRHINI (GRAHAMSTOWN)

They always [called] me bad names such as "istabanee," "mofee," "domi quay." I became a street fighter. When someone was calling me mofee or whatever, I just got angry and took hold of anything that was in front of me and made it a weapon and beat them just to clear the air.

I don't take hormones. I love my body as it is. In my village, I can't just go out dressed as a woman. They will do something bad to me. They will make a plan with their group. What to do about this boy, me, the mofee. They would take me to the Bush and rape me. So in this place, I find it hard to just be me. Transgenders are being beaten by men. They take you to somewhere else and beat you or even kill you.

I failed my grade 12. There's nothing stopping me from going back. I wanted to go to another school, but I didn't have time. My mind said to me it's too late, I'm too old, I can't go back to school. My mom and my father don't have a job. They don't get paid enough money for me to go back to school. School is not free. I want to get a job so I can pay myself. Maybe it's four thousand rand per year. I just want to finish my grade 12 so I can go to university.

I identify as transgender, but people here only know me as "gay." My family knows what a gay person is. But my father is . . . I think he will be harsh when I tell him, "Dad, I'm dating the same sex." I could say that my dad and I are friends, but I think we would be separated by a fight if I told him.

I do want to be loved like other people are loved. I see them, they are happy; they are doing good things when they are together, when they are working together, like kissing, talking, and buying gifts for each other.

IN HER OWN WRITING

As I was growing up, I did not know where to turn. I grew up on a farm facing bad and the good, because in the olden days, on a farm as a boy I had to do hard work. I did that just to please my parents. At that time my parents had only two children, my sister and me. My parents had wishes for their second-born child to be a boy. When my body started to tell me whom I was attracted to, I can say that was a hard time for me. By the time we were playing as youngsters, I mostly chose to play the mother part, and some of my friends were at loss, but I kept on doing the same. They got tired of me and started to call me names, which made me feel unwanted. I was so young and naive then, I didn't know how to respond. I used to take everything that was in front of me and make it into a weapon. My parents got a house here in [eRhini], and we moved out of the farm. By moving to town, I thought I would live a better life and not have to face the challenges I faced on the farm.

We moved into town during the school holidays, and many kids were on holiday just to get fresh air, meet their loved ones. Early on the following day I woke up to look for a friend. I got lucky. I found someone who was just like me. It was the first time I had met a person who was like me. He was dressing like a lady, acting like a lady, everything about him was ladylike.

The holiday ended and the school reopened. My first day at school was the best day, I enjoyed meeting new teachers and new friends, but I did not know what was coming for me in the following days. I went home after school, and we were given homework by our class teacher. At school the following day, teachers and schoolmates started to notice who I was, and a few of my schoolmates frowned, started gossiping and even laughing at me. I couldn't help myself, I cried and tried to get them away from me. I got myself help when I met Mrs. Ntlumbini, who was my Xhosa teacher. She stood up for my rights, and that is how I could continue my schooling.

One day I woke up thinking of visiting a school friend of mine. I went to her home not knowing that her parents were home. I knocked and the father opened [the door]. I greeted him, but he didn't even bother to greet me back. He just asked what I wanted. I told him that I came to visit his daughter. He said to me, his child didn't have friends who are boys. I tried to reveal myself to him just to make him see that I was like a girl, but that didn't help me. Things got even worse. He then asked, "Are you one of those boys who disgust me, who are with other boys?" I didn't answer that stupid question, I ignored him. I walked out of his yard, and we shouted at each other, and everyone near us heard everything, and people of the community turned their back on me, saying that I'm [a] spoiled brat. They were mad at me. I was raised by both parents, but the difficulties were not that bad. My mom used to tell me when people called me "mofee," "No, my boy, don't stress, just ignore them, get over it." That's why I say she's also the one [who] made me stronger.

I came out of the closet at a late age, and I exaggerated things because I was living a lie. Some things I did, I did them just to please my father. I know that my father will never accept me if I tell him that I am gay, because he's a Christian. By the look of things, he doesn't mind my dressing like a lady, bringing my girlfriends home; he never lectures me about those things— the only thing that can make him throw me out is to hear that his son is gay.

With all these bad things I faced in life, they made me strong. I can do whatever makes my father happy; I'm okay with that, because when he is happy I am also happy. I can live a lie just to make my father happy.

—November 2015

THANDILE SHOWS US HER NEW PUPPY, HERE WITH THANDILE'S MOTHER AND LITTLE SISTER. ERHINI, NOVEMBER 2015

# ON BELEM STREET

# On Belem Street

SINALO STAMPER

EXTENSION 9, eRhini (GRAHAMSTOWN)

I am an outgoing person, very bubbly person. I love making new friends. I love going out. I love having fun. I'm twenty-two years old, and I'm from Grahamstown. I was born here.

In the past I identified myself as a male who is gay. I learned the difference between a gay person and a trans woman; now that I know the difference, I identify myself as a trans woman. I used to live with both my parents. My parents are unmarried, and my dad passed away three years ago. I live with my mom now, and my brother and my family just accept me the way I am. They never had a problem with me playing with dolls, playing with girls. At school people were calling me names like "mofee," but I have gotten used to it. I don't really mind it anymore. I went to a Catholic school. The priest was so much fun. Totally fun.

When I turned eighteen, my dad asked me if I wanted to go to the Bush. He could see that I was not like the other boys. And I told him, I can't, it's not my life. If I'm going to be circumcised, it's going to have to be the healthy way. At the men's clinic. I was born like this. It's natural. I even have breasts, and they're natural. I don't take hormones. [I'm] dating someone now. I can't say he is straight, because he's dating me. But I think I'm bisexual. To me, he is straight because I feel as a woman. And I sure [would] like to get married and then adopt maybe two kids one day. A boy and a girl.

Grahamstown is such a small town, it doesn't have that many trans women. As years go by, I think people are actually becoming more accepting of us. They know we're here to stay, nothing is going to change, so they might as well accept us or they would be wasting their time. I've personally never faced bad things other than just stupid insults.

—November 2015

SIYA AND SINALO ON BELEM STREET, ERHINI, NOVEMBER 2015

## SIYAMTHANDA

My family is very supportive. They accepted me from day one. They never say anything wrong. I identify myself as gay, and I identify as a woman. I'm not quite female yet. I haven't changed my identity and my gender. I have never met any difficulties in Grahamstown. I never met such terrible challenges like people insulting me; they do call me "mofee," but I don't pay attention to them because at the end of the day, they're not going to give me anything. What prevents me from being a woman now, from becoming a woman, [is] the expenses. I don't have that kind of money to buy those things, the medication to grow breasts and stop growing [a] beard and that type of thing.

I grew up with my cousins, they are all girls. We all played with dolls, but when you are young, you play with everything, you play with boys, you play with girls. At that time, because I was so young I didn't have in my mind that I was a girl. I think I was in grade 4 when I knew, at the time I was in the school choir. I was singing. I started to realize that I'm different. I told my mum that I don't think I have feelings for girls. So she asked me: how do I know that? She said I should think about it, that I am confused. But she gave me a chance. My uncle didn't like it at first, but he ended up loving me for who I was. He supported me all the way.

Circumcision was a choice for me. You can go to the clinic if you want to get circumcised. You can also go to the hospital. You don't have to go to the Bush and stay alone for all those weeks. I think that's torture. I don't think it's a good idea to go to the Bush. To stay those weeks without eating and do those things, eat that food without salt for four weeks. My grandma used to tell me not to attend those places, to take part in those kinds of tribal things.

I wear pants for work. I've never worn a dress. I think I would like to develop breasts. I'm not sure yet, but I think so.

I'd like to give a home to those children who don't have a proper home; I want to get married and adopt children. I'm dating straight people. I don't do gay people. If it's necessary, I tell people about myself, but if it's not necessary, I don't tell. If a man thinks that I'm a girl, I correct him. I'm not a girl; I'm gay, but I'm transgender. I don't even have breasts, so why would you think I am a girl? I haven't met a man who has a problem with that. Nothing bad has happened. Maybe if I change my destination. Maybe if I go to Cape Town; most of those terrible things, gay bash[ing], they happen in Cape Town, but here, never.

I belong to the Roman Catholic Church. I can dress like this, with jeans and T-shirt in church; you can wear anything in my church. Whatever you are comfortable with.

—November 2015

SINALO AND SIYA OUTSIDE THEIR HOME, eRHINI, NOVEMBER 2015

YOU CAN TAKE MY PICTURE

LUTHO AT S.H.E.'S OFFICES IN EMONTI, APRIL 2014: A MISUNDERSTANDING LED US TO MISS OUR INTERVIEW WITH LUTHO. LUTHO WAS ONE OF THE FIRST WOMEN WE PHOTOGRAPHED FOR THIS PROJECT WHEN WE CAME TO SOUTH AFRICA. LUTHO LIVES ON HER OWN IN EMONTI

GOD KNOWS WHO I AM

# God Knows Who I Am

## LINDANI (BJ) HLABA

D-SECTION, DUNCAN VILLAGE

Last night my brothers were going out. I have three brothers. When they came back, I was sleeping on the floor, because I have to show them respect, because they are my big brothers. They sleep in beds. They said to me, "Just wake up. Wake up." I said, "Wake up? Where am I going to go? It's late." Then they shouted at me. And kicked me out. I was crying last night, really crying. I slept outside like a little kid.

I've got a big problem with my family, especially my brothers. They don't like the way I am. They tease me each and every day. They don't beat me. But when I am cooking for them or when I'm reading or doing homework, they say, "Clean up. Clean up. Clean up. Faster. Dishes. Go and fetch the waters." I say to them, "I'm reading." They say, "We are saying to you, go and fetch the waters." Like a respectful child, I take the bucket and go fetch the water.

I feel like a girl. I don't feel like a man. I like kitchen jobs, and I like making people happy. They call me mofee, transgender. That was a problem. A big one. They were giving me names. They were beating me. The children at school. The teachers told me to ignore them, but they just kept teasing me. My parents don't give a damn about it. They liked what they did to me. My parents look at me like I'm an idiot.

God knows who I am. My pastor says to keep being the way I am and believe in God. God knows what he's doing. Some people like me; some people don't. The people who love me, they say, "Oh good girl. We really know that you want to be a girl." People who don't like me, they say, "Oh, oh no. You won't be a girl anymore. Just be the way that God made you," and they shout at me.

I am nineteen years old now. After grade nine I was very stressed—my family didn't like who I was, and before they went

*Ubuntu* means to care about someone,

to care about everyone,

but when I go out,

I don't feel the *Ubuntu* anymore.

*Ubuntu* was here when I grew up.

But the more I grow up,

people don't know *Ubuntu*.

They don't care about other people.

So you see,

now people don't care about one another,

so there is no *Ubuntu*.

BJ AT HOME IN DUNCAN VILLAGE, APRIL 2014

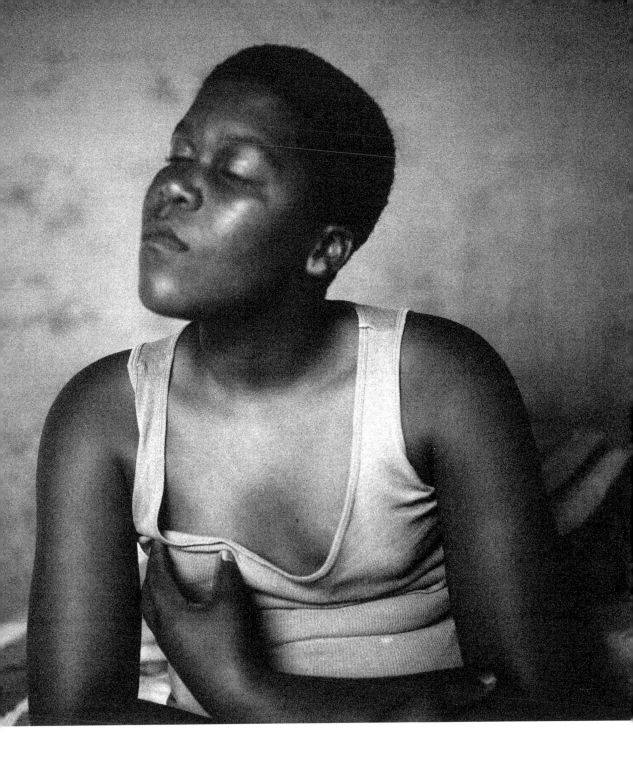

to work in the morning, they would say to me, "Don't go to school. Check on the babies. Be a babysitter." My grandma used to say that. Some days my parents would support my grandma, and other days they wouldn't support her, because they say I'm a child and I don't know what I'm doing. I need the support from them to teach me good and bad.

I'm studying very well. I'm working hard. I like school, and I want to pass my exams and then go to university to do my journalism. Because I see some people who don't like transgenders and gays, I want to gain some knowledge why they don't like transgenders and gays. I want to tell the rest of the world what gay is, what transgender is, and they should like us because we are people.

I am going to get circumcised. I feel so scared. My family last year, they said I must go to the Mountain in December, but I refused because I said to them, "I don't feel well enough to go to the mountain. Let me go when I'm ready." Later I told them, "Okay, fine. Now I'm ready to go to the Mountain." But it is really because they are forcing me. I want to make them happy, although they don't make me happy.

I'm a girl inside. I want to do hormones when I'm ready. When I have my own place. My own things. When I'm out of my family so that they can't judge me, when they can't tell me what to do and what not to do. I think I can leave my family when I pass my grade.

BJ GOT KICKED OUT OF HER HOME SHORTLY AFTER WE INTERVIEWED HER IN APRIL 2014. LEIGH ANN AND HER COLLEAGUES AT S.H.E. HELPED BJ GET A PLACE TO LIVE. WE BRIEFLY MET BJ WHEN WE CAME BACK TO SOUTH AFRICA IN NOVEMBER 2015. SHE HAD MOVED BACK HOME.

I was in a relationship once for two weeks. It was fun. When we first met, I was walking with my friends. Once he asked me, do I have a moment. I said "Yes." Then he said, "I love you so much." I said, "I love you, too." The following day, he went to say the same thing to someone else. I said, "What are you doing, this is my friend." He was not the person I thought he was. I realized that he's not good for me. And I just left him.

*Ubuntu* means to care about someone, to care about everyone, but when I go out, I don't feel the *Ubuntu* anymore. *Ubuntu* was here when I grew up. But the more I grow up, people don't know *Ubuntu*. They don't care about other people. So you see, now people don't care about one another, so there is no *Ubuntu*.

—April 2014

# THE SUIT OF MANHOOD

# The Suit of Manhood
## SIYAKIHANYA

MDANTSANE, EASTERN CAPE

They [my family] forced me to have a circumcision. I had to attend circumcision school because everybody knew I was a male. It's not a choice for us. You have to go to the Bush. I came back from the Bush, dressed in a suit. The Suit of Manhood.

I would like to run my own business. I am a hairstylist. I don't want any children. I don't want to take hormones. I know I am a male on the outside, so I don't have to have breasts. I'm trans, so what? I like the way I am, no bum, hips, or breasts. I like it this way.

People call me "Sissy" now. Like in "Sister." I no longer wear a dress, I just wear skinny jeans. My boyfriend lives in Cape Town. I've visited him once. He keeps calling me. I don't want to marry him because I know him, and I know he can cheat.

I noticed that I was a girl when I was two or three years old. I wanted to wear a dress and play with girls. My brother has a problem with me. My father did not accept me. But then a friend of my father came to my father and told him, "This is your son. As long as he listens to what you say in this house, he will be your son. So leave him in peace." After that he accepted it. My father and my mom are separated now.

My mother is working. We have a close relationship. My mother noticed when I was young, that I was different. We didn't have the word *trans* then. We only had *gay* and *mofee*. I am a boy, but a girl on the inside. I was teased at school, but not bullied. The community here where I live doesn't have a problem with me, because there are many gays around. I have always hung out with other girls. I would play with girls and gays.

—April 2014

SIYAKIHANYA OUTSIDE THE HOME THAT SHE SHARES WITH HER MOTHER AND SISTER. MDANTSANE, APRIL 2014

People call me "Sissy" now.

Like in "Sister."

I no longer wear a dress,

I just wear skinny jeans.

SIYAKIHANYA'S HOME KITCHEN. MDANTSANE, APRIL 2014

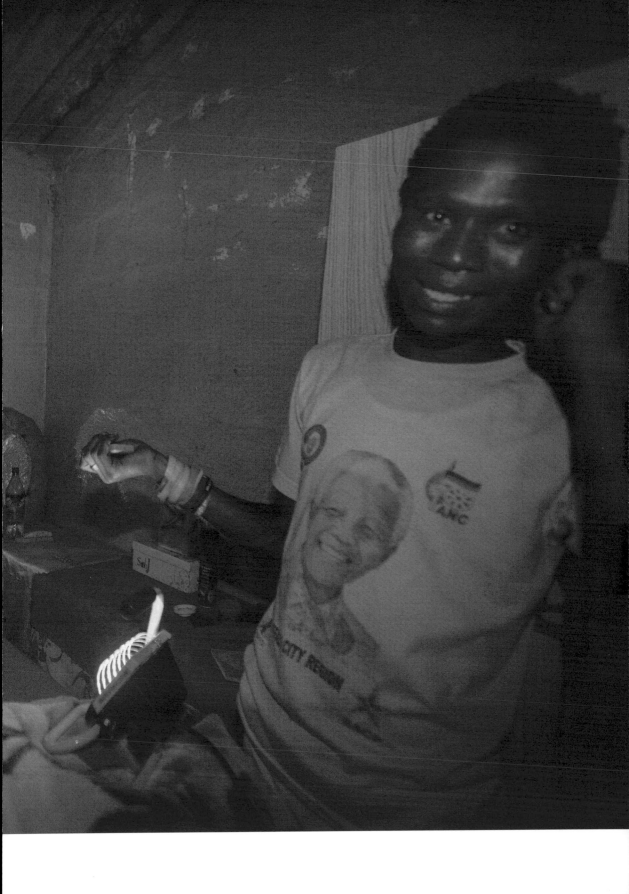

PREVIOUS SPREAD: SIYAKIHANYA IN HER BEDROOM WITH THABISA MOYIKWA (RIGHT), WHO IS TRANSLATING FOR US FROM XHOSA

I DON'T THINK GOD

CREATED THIS

# I Don't Think God Created This
## SIZWE

EQONCE (KING WILLIAMSTOWN)

I think it was in 2009, when I started to know myself as a trans. I've only had four boyfriends in my life. When I had a boyfriend, sometimes it was nice. Sometimes it was not nice at all. My boyfriend was too jealous and always in charge of me. He would just ask too many questions. One of my men took me for a girl because he loved me. He treated me like a girl.

I went to circumcision school in 2011. It was nice, it was good there, but you also felt the pain when you were in the Mountain [the Bush]. No one forced me to go to the Mountain, but I told myself that I should go, since my parents think I am a boy. They never noticed that I am transgender.

The family's treating me well. My sisters are treating me well because they know that I grew up trans. So there's no way that they can treat me bad. They take me as their other sister. And my brothers, sometimes they joke about me.

I left school because of lack of memory. It takes a long time [for me] to learn and remember. I would love to work, no matter what kind of work. I would be so proud of it because I want to work hard and have money in the bank.

Being trans, where do I think this comes from? It's a feeling that you have inside. I feel the way I feel and have felt from an early stage. I don't believe that God created this. It's something that comes from my heart.

—April 2014

Being trans,

where do I think this comes from?

It's a feeling that you have inside.

I feel the way I feel

and have felt from an early stage.

I don't believe

that God created this.

It's something that comes

from my heart.

SIZWE OUTSIDE HER FRIEND'S HOUSE IN EQONCE, APRIL 2014

SIZWE ON HER FRIEND'S BED IN EQONCE, APRIL 2014

THERE IS NOTHING WRONG

WITH YONELA

# There Is Nothing Wrong
# With Yonela

## YONELA

eQONCE (KING WILLIAMSTOWN)

I was born in East London. When I was a year and eight
months old, I went to stay with my grandmother, my father's
mother, in Alice. So that's where I grew up. After I finished high
school, I came and stayed with my aunt in King Williamtown.
That's where I'm working now, and I'm still staying with her.

Kindergarten was good. First grade, yeah. At that time I
was always like a happy person. Everything I did was with girls.
People would tease me, say things like, "Hi, you playing with
girls. You are a mofee." I asked my mother to remove me from
that school, and she took me to go to another school in Alice.
When I told my grandmother about the teasing, she said she
was going to remove me from that school, as well. She'd go to
the teachers and tell them, "They're teasing my child. They are
saying he's a mofee." She didn't have a problem with me playing
with girls, and we would cook and bake together, my grandmother and me. I am a good cook now.

At this new school I made friends, three friends who were
also transgender. We talked about boys who were born girls. At
the age of four I felt like I was a girl, I knew already at that age.
And that I was attracted to boys.

My father was married for the second time, and his wife was
staying with my grandmother; he was not. He was working in
"PE," Port Elizabeth. She and I were close, we still are, so I told
her what I was feeling. I was around thirteen then. The only
thing she said to me, "I don't think your father will like what
I'm hearing now." She told me I shouldn't tell my dad, he's a
very strict person. I should keep it to myself. If I have a problem,
I should come and speak to her. If he was around on holidays,
I wouldn't go out and play because he would ask why do I play
with girls. I should go on and play with boys, because I am a

YONELA WITH HER GIRLFRIENDS. eQONCE, APRIL 2014

boy. So I had to stay in the house, not go out.

If I was joking in the house, he would look at me and say, "What are you doing? You're not a girl, you're [a] boy. Stop acting this way," and he would get very angry. And he would hit me. If I'd go out and come back late, then he would hit me: "Where have you been?!"

I didn't really know my mother until I was about fourteen. She came to me, she introduced herself. And I would go with her for holidays. My mother, she is a Christian and attends the Assemblies of God. She would tell me what to wear, and she would take me to church to have me changed; she tried. I knew where this was going, and we started to not get along. But I got along with her sisters. Their church was the Church of Jesus Christ of the Latter-day Saints. The elders would visit us, and they would say they were going to pray for me. But my aunts didn't have a problem with me and were supportive. They would even confront my mother. My church now is Wesley Methodist, where there are other transgender people I know. But we are in hiding. I am not surprised that I know so many transgenders. The minister is very good and nice. He has never said anything to offend me, and I have never heard him talk about gay people in a bad way. I go on Sundays and Wednesday. Wednesday is the girls' night.

On my Dad's side they are not religious. When he got sick and stopped working, he went to Alice and stayed at my grandma's, who had by then passed away. I went there and stayed with him. That's when we started getting along. He didn't have a problem with me then. He told me, "No, I didn't want you to be this way, but it was more that I didn't want to act like I'm letting you do this way. At that time you were still very young, two or three; you would go to a shop and cry for a dress. I thought actually you was going to . . . change, but now I see you don't change. I don't have a problem with that."

After I passed my metric [exams], my father got sick[er]. He had kidney problems and also had pneumonia from HIV. He

*Ubuntu* means to give,

to give to someone.

If you don't have a pen and I have a pen,

I should give you my pen.

If I have bread,

I should share with you.

*Ubuntu* is very much in my culture.

Now at home we have maize,

it's that time of the year.

I will be giving them to every household

in the village,

and they who grow potatoes,

in return,

will share theirs with the village.

YONELA SAYS SHE IS HAPPY WITH WHO SHE IS,
BUT NEEDS HELP TO REMOVE BODY AND FACIAL
HAIR. EQONCE, APRIL 2014

passed away in January 2011, three years ago. I miss them both, my father and my grandmother. When others in the family were saying I needed to see a psychologist, my grandmother would say, "There is nothing wrong with Yonela."

*Ubuntu* means to give, to give to someone. If you don't have a pen and I have a pen, I should give you my pen. If I have bread, I should share with you. *Ubuntu* is very much in my culture. Now at home we have maize, it's that time of the year. I will be giving them to every household in the village, and they who grow potatoes, in return, will share theirs with the village.

## Too much hair

I've got two names actually. My mother gave me Yonela. My father gave me Siabonga. Then when I was in grade 2, that's when I changed my name. I used Yonela only. Most Yonelas are females. My mom gave it to me when I was born. I don't know if it means anything.

I was attracted to boys [from] when I was nine or ten. I thought a lot about boys when I was around fourteen years old. I had my first sexual experience when I was fourteen, with a boy of sixteen. We stayed together until I was nineteen.

When I was nineteen and came to East London, my friends were staying by the beachfront. Then I never wanted to go home. Because I was around people I could share with what I was feeling. I stayed here for about a year. My parents didn't know where I was. At least I could wear what I wanted to wear. I wore skirts. I was comfortable with the people I was around. But my aunt, she investigated one day and she came over to the house that we were staying in. They took me home.

I was taking hormones I got from my friend when I was staying in East London. I don't know how to describe it. It felt good. My other friends are not hairy like me, and that's why I wanted to take hormones. I don't want to have hair like this. If I wanted to wear something short, I couldn't because of my hair. I have to shave my legs first. But I think I'm comfortable with the way that I am now. The doctors here say that before you take hormones you should consult a therapist. And especially if you want to do genital reconstruction therapies or some part of it, you need to see a [therapist]. I want to have surgery but not now. I want to continue and concentrate on my education first. If I had the chance, I would want to have surgery as well as hormones. I think it is available now in South Africa, in Cape Town.

I'm happy with who I am, I feel very good. I want to go back to school next year . . . to do fashion design. But there aren't any good schools around here. I was thinking of going to my other aunt I get along with. She lives in Johannesburg. I get along with her two younger kids, but the older one, we don't get along. My aunt tried to take me to a psychologist in East London. But I haven't seen my aunt in maybe four or five years. We don't communicate. Just like my mother, we don't communicate. I last saw my mother at my dad's funeral.

—April 2014

# Epilogue: Being Trans & Xhosa in post-Apartheid South Africa

The beginning of life starts because of another set of lives. But our very, very first beginning (biblically described as Eve) derives from much scientific discovery and is said to have happened in East Africa, not too far from where the Xhosas and their neighbors live. All non-Africans' DNA can be traced back to one single population in Africa from roughly two hundred thousand years ago.[1] Genes from hundreds of indigenous people like the Basques, Pygmies, Mayans, Bedouins, Sherpas, Cree Indians, and Aboriginal Australians can attest to this.

Henry Louis Gates Jr. wrote in "History the Slaveholders Wanted Us to Forget"[2] that Africa is also filled with kings and queens, real and magical kingdoms, and rival empires, along with hundreds of ethnic groups, rich cultures, and languages. Africa has an incredibly interesting history spanning thousands of years, with which we share ancestors and humanity. "Perhaps it shouldn't surprise us that ideas about Africans and their supposed lack of history and culture were used to justify the enslavement of millions of Africans throughout the New World," Gates writes. "What is surprising is that these ideas persisted well into the 20th century, among white and black Americans alike."

Today Africa still has at least three thousand different spoken languages. Nigeria alone has five hundred, and most Africans are bilingual and multilingual. With fifty-four countries and thousands of ethnic groups, this continent is unique and astonishingly diverse.

---

1 Carl Zimmer, "A Single Migration from Africa Populated the World, Studies Find," *New York Times*, September 21, 2016.

2 Henry Louis Gates Jr., "History the Slaveholders Wanted Us to Forget," *New York Times*, February 4, 2017.

Back in our privileged bubble called Berkeley, we miss being able to see our new friends and colleagues; we are affirmed by our contact with them and feel a deep sense of gratitude. These women on the Eastern Cape, transgender activists that they are—by sharing their stories—should force us to reexamine our prejudices. They should urge us to fill in gaps in our knowledge, from our cloistered first world assumptions that they are passive victims of the history we have been taught. They can teach us about resiliency and that social empowerment can allow them to stand tall and embrace their essential humanity after hundreds of years of depredation, which not only robbed and continues to rob them of their continent's wealth, but even their sense that it is in fact theirs. We are learning just how deep generations of lies made systemic by colonial plunder can go. They are pressing us to take on uncomfortable discussions of our roles, or to find that we will be left in that infamous "dust bin of history."

As long as we cannot confront our truths, there are no truths.

All Leigh Ann asked from us and others in the West is that we give back to the community. Not by way of money but by spreading knowledge about their cause. They have been repeatedly disappointed before. Researchers, students, journalists come to collect stories about "the poor" and go back to the West, never to be seen again. We hope that with this book, we give something back, as it is in their voices that the change can be made, and this book can contribute to their continuous fight for freedom. They were more than pleased to share of themselves whenever we asked. We never felt any resentment or any attempts to instill guilt. The women of the Eastern Cape only gave us the *Ubuntu* that they were born with, the *Ubuntu* that was there from the beginning, passed on in their genes, in their blood, from life long lived before their foremothers were born.

—Kris Lyseggen and Herb Schreier
March 1, 2017

# S.H.E.

Founded in 2010, S.H.E. (Social, Health, and Empowerment) is a feminist
collective for and by African trans and intersex women to create greater
awareness of their issues at a community level, advocate for health services,
and involve and pressure policy makers to fulfill health commitments to
their community, including conducting health research and ensuring legal
and human rights are applied to the lives of transgender and intersex women.
S.H.E. wishes more than to just align with the feminist movement: "We are
not hoping to reinvent feminism; instead we are seeking to expand feminism
to recognize the problems of African trans and intersex within the feminist
sphere." S.H.E. was established as a response to the gender imbalance in the
trans African movement and as a response to an African women's (and
feminist) movement that often excludes trans and intersex women.

## Kris Lyseggen

Norwegian-born writer and documentary photographer Kris Lyseggen is based in California, Italy, and Norway. Her previous nonfiction books, *The Boy Who Was Not a Lesbian* and *The Women of San Quentin*, convey the prejudice and ignorance transgender people experience and the horrendous treatment that transgender people undergo in the US prison system. *The Women of San Quentin* won an IPPY award for best LGBT nonfiction in 2016. Kris has published, presented, and exhibited her work in Bangkok, Birmingham, Oslo, Indiana, Hamburg, California, and London. Her long-term projects have taken her to the Middle East, Thailand, Alabama, Morocco, Cuba, Kenya, Georgia, and South Africa, as well as all corners of Europe. Trained as a journalist and photographer in Oslo, UK, Bangkok, and San Francisco, Kris' calling is to tell true stories, to give individuals a voice, and to create images that advance social justice. She is mostly using a medium format 120-film Rolleiflex Twin lens.

## Herb Schreier

Herb Schreier is a child psychiatrist at UCSF Benioff Children's Hospital in Oakland, California, and the coauthor of *Hurting for Love* about parents with Munchausen Syndrome by Proxy. Herb grew up in the Bronx, New York, and went to Albert Einstein Medical School. He has presented his work and participated in collaborations for several decades around the world, and helped to establish a program in child psychiatry in Tirana, Albania. Herb has been an active member of international transgender communities to advance mental health care from the early days as increasing numbers of transgender children were asking for support, and has planted the seeds for one of the largest gender-creative and nonconforming, open-walls clinics for children called Mind The Gap in the San Francisco Bay area. His interest and training are in the well-being of children, with particular experience in cognitive and developmental disorders in the very young such as autism, Tourette's, ADD, gender identity, and Obsessive-Compulsive Disorder.

# Enkosi [Thank you]

A special thanks to all the women who shared their stories in this book who guided and supported us, who bravely participated with the hope that the future would be easier and safer for their comrades and those who come after.

To Leigh Ann van der Merwe, a pioneer woman of transfeminism who showed us the way to Eastern Cape. To Thabisa Moyikwa and Phiwe Ngcingi for their extraordinary help in shepherding us around places we could never have found otherwise; who so warmly and effortlessly translated, guided and educated us. To S.H.E. and all the wonderful people we met working in South Africa including Simon Pickstone-Taylor — thank you for your unwavering support to the transgender communities.

To the book team of wonders; Bob Aufuldish, Paula Dragosh, the Photolab in Berkeley, Debra Kalmon, Shirley Sheffield, Ben Zlotkin at Edition One Books, and Editcetera.

To Jorunn Solli, Tekstuniverset and Katrine Storebø for creative, collegial, win-win womanship. To Sidsel Stenbak who became a great source of support.

To Nicola Masini, Constantin Catalin Baulau, Phillip Jones, Roy Santi and Heather Formaini who are making the transition to our new home in a new country so interesting and smooth. For guidance and much more, Fresh! White, Hope Frye and MJ Bogatin. To our family for their love and willingness to go deeper. To Abby, Jake, Mathea, Marie and Mikkel who give us hope. To all our friends and neighbors who have read every book we have made and given us feedback.

—Kris Lyseggen and Herb Schreier